Vacation Houses

An International Survey

Karl Kaspar

Vacation Houses

An International Survey

Frederick A. Praeger, Publishers
New York · Washington

BOOKS THAT MATTER

Published in the United States of America in 1967
by Frederick A. Praeger, Inc., Publishers
111 Fourth Avenue, New York, N.Y. 10003
All rights reserved
Copyright in Stuttgart in 1967 by Verlag Gerd Hatje, Stuttgart, Germany
Library of Congress Catalog Card Number: 67–17762
Translation into English: E. Rockwell
Printed in Germany

Contents

Inhalt

The wide variety offered by the fifty international examples illustrated in this book make it difficult to define the criteria by which the holiday or vacation house can be distinguished from buildings of a similar character. At the upper end of the scale, it is not far removed from the 'villa' type country house, which in layout and amenities is almost identical with a town house. At the lower end, it is closely related to the simply equipped weekend cottage. The border line is perhaps most clearly manifested by the basic shelters – hunting lodges and ski huts – designed for short stays only, which give little more than weather protection and are generally without any architectural pretensions.

Comparisons between the vacation house and tent or trailer can be dismissed not only on the grounds of cost, but in difference of purpose and standard of equipment. Ultimately the choice between these forms of holiday accommodation is a matter of personal preference. There are arguments on both sides. There is little point in weighing the mobility of tent and trailer against the immobility of the house. The larger area of the house offers scope for a greater range of activities and a clear separation into areas for day-time and night-time use. The standard of sanitary equipment and other domestic installations is limited only by cost and individual demands for comfort; and the clearly established property rights are likely to ensure greater privacy.

But whether tent, trailer, or house, each has one feature in common. Most holiday and vacation activities take place out-of-doors; in fact, outdoor living is normally more important than indoor living. It is only in wet weather, when the family may be shut in for hours or days at a time, that the decisive advantage of a house becomes fully apparent. Then the convenience of adequate indoor amenities is appreciated, especially if there are several rooms.

That is why present trends tend to veer away from the mere roof-over-the-head principle—the basic hut—to solutions that provide enough space for indoor activities. From this point of view the Japanese 'plastic egg' (figs. 1–3) meets the very minimum demands of a holiday house at best, even though its insulation and electrical and sanitary equipment are technically of high quality. In such a confined space, the occupants can be expected to live together amicably only if their habits are very similar, and if they are willing to exert a considerable measure of self-discipline.

The space available for various activities, or the extent to which makeshift arrangements are acceptable, may help define the fluid border line between the vacation house and the weekend cottage. For an occasional over-night stay, drawing water from the well, making do with oil lamps, or enjoying a menu without a refrigerator, can be an interesting change from normal routine, but is apt to become a nuisance if extended over several weeks. In other words, the equipment in a vacation house must meet more exacting demands, since living informally is by no means tantamount to renouncing all comforts. As this attitude is increasingly adopted by the designers of many weekend cottages, the differences between house and cottage are becoming fewer. The present book, therefore, is confined to houses that do not have primitive equipment and are therefore suitable for a prolonged stay.

Despite differences, the examples presented in this book have one characteristic in common: they all form the architectural frame for a way of living different from the routine life of a town dweller. The essential features of this sort of existence are close contact with nature and informality. This is reflected not only in the relaxing change from routine but in the way normal conventions are set aside—an attitude, however, that is not identical with a sentimental back-to-nature philosophy, now, incidentally, on the wane.

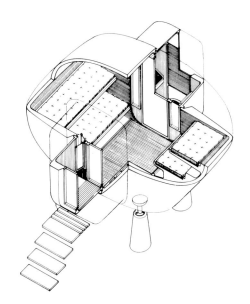

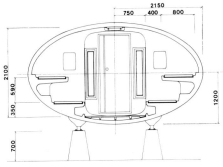

1–3. Perspective, elevation and longitudinal section of a prefabricated ski hut consisting of a 3 mm thick, fibreglass reinforced plastic shell. (Design: GK Industrial Association, Tokyo; Manufacturer: Kometsu Plastic Industry Ltd.)

1–3. Perspektive, Ansicht und Längsschnitt einer vorfabrizierten Skihütte mit 3 mm starker fiberglasverstärkter Kunststoffschale.

6

The holiday or vacation house is particularly suitable for families with children, who do not want to fit in with hotel routine, yet are averse to the scantier comforts of camping. To such families the holiday house offers an ideal environment—it gives ample scope for personal moods and almost any hobby, while enabling the members of the family to live more closely together than during times of normal work and school routine.

These factors, together with the shortage of domestic labour, have a definite bearing on the planning of the house. The layout should allow, as far as possible, free movement between indoors and outdoors (figs. 4, 5). It should provide easy access to open space, as well as a variety of wholly or partly covered outdoor sitting places (figs. 6–10)—in the shape of loggias, balconies, terraces, or pergolas—that form an extension to the inside space and provide shelter from sun and wind.

The layout should allow the living room (fig. 19) sufficient space for subdivision into separate areas, at least for eating and sitting (figs. 12–13), yet leaving the bedrooms large enough to provide a day-time retreat. It is important to provide adequate sound insulation for the children's bedrooms or situate them so that the adults do not have to restrict their evening conversation to whispers. When larger holiday houses need additional space for guests, it has often been found convenient to group these rooms into a self-contained wing or on a separate floor.

Attention should be paid also to the arrangement of the kitchen area even where this amounts to no more than a kitchenette (fig. 11) or free standing unit (fig. 13) of stove, work top and sink. It is rare for the kitchen to be completely separated from the living

4. Each room has direct access from outside; the bedroom is reached through the wind-protected porch, the living room through the balcony at the end (Page 51).
5. All the rooms are connected by sliding doors with the sun decks which are placed at a lower level along the sides (Page 44).

4. Jeder Raum ist direkt mit dem Freien verbunden: die Schlafräume über die windgeschützte Terrasse, der Wohnraum über den Balkon vor der Stirnseite (Seite 51).
5. Schiebetüren öffnen alle Räume auf den gedeckten Umgang mit den tiefer liegenden Sonnendecks auf den Längsseiten (Seite 44).

6–10. Various possibilities of creating covered or open terraces close to the house. Fig. 6: Passage covered by a post-supported roof and forming an extension of the living room when the sliding door is opened (Page 28). Fig. 7: Projecting platform, protected on the sides by the tent-shaped roof (Page 134). Fig. 8: The sliding doors are pushed back so that living room and sun deck are combined (Page 48). Fig. 9: Sun deck with shingle balustrade to ensure privacy (Page 126). Fig. 10: Dining terrace covered by a pergola (Page 82).

6–10. Verschiedene Möglichkeiten für überdeckte oder offene Freisitzplätze im Hausbereich. Abb. 6: Laufgang unter vorspringendem Dach als Erweiterung des Wohnbereichs bei geöffneter Schiebetür (Seite 28). Abb. 7: Auskragende Plattform mit seitlichem Windschutz durch das zeltförmige Dach (Seite 134). Abb. 8: Zurückgeschobene Schiebetüren verbinden Wohnraum und Sonnendeck (Seite 48). Abb. 9: Sonnendeck mit Schindelbrüstung als Sichtschutz (Seite 126). Abb. 10: Pergolaüberdachter Eßplatz im Freien (Seite 82).

11. Kitchenette forming part of the living room so that the housewife is not isolated in her kitchen (Page 86).

11. Zum Wohnraum offene Kochnische, um die Hausfrau nicht im Küchenbereich zu isolieren (Seite 86).

room, since this arrangement isolates the housewife from the family activities. Among the American examples, especially, layouts with island-type or wall-type kitchen units predominate (fig. 14).

In winter sports areas, cloakrooms near the entrance (fig. 16) may serve as a room for drying wet clothing or as storage space for skis and other sports gear, fishing tackle or gum boots. Last but not least, planning should ensure that the housewife is relieved of domestic drudgery as much as possible. A logical layout, which saves unnecessary steps and physical effort, can ease her task as much as the selection of finishes that are easy to maintain; carpeting a house in the dunes where sand is carried in all the time would be as unsuitable as parquet flooring in a ski hut.

Naturally such considerations vary between countries and regions. Spanish and Latin American examples often have several rooms or even an entire wing for domestic staff, since a large labour supply is normally available throughout the year. In the U. S., architects and clients are concerned with reducing housework to a minimum, and labour saving equipment, such as a refrigerator, washing machine, and similar electrical appliances, are taken for granted.

For a house on the Mediterranean, the most effective protection against the heat is provided by solid stone or concrete walls (fig. 17). On the other hand, the heat of the sun is highly welcome in a Finnish timber house (fig. 18), and wind protection by screen walls on the exposed side of a beach cottage is as necessary as snow protection for the roof of a house in high mountains.

A correlation also exists between building density and house type. On a site of several acres, a house can be opened up in all directions (fig. 20). A narrow plot on a closely built up area such as Long Island calls for a more introverted layout (fig. 21), which often makes it difficult to reconcile the desire for outdoor playing and sitting facilities with the need to ensure privacy.

Despite such qualifications, the examples in the present volume point to certain basic types of house design and layout with certain clearly recognizable features. The type most frequently met is the box-shaped bungalow on a rectangular plan (fig. 22) divided into two halves (fig. 23), one containing the bedrooms, the other containing the living room and in many cases a covered terrace.

The link between the two halves is provided by the service units, i. e. W. C., shower, bath, and kitchen. The roof, normally flat, is generally cantilevered, at least on the side facing the sun or prevailing winds, so as to protect the windows and terrace against the midday sun and driving rain. This basic house, which needs no more than simple strip or pile foundations, is economical as well as adaptable. If the site slopes (fig. 24), levels can be adjusted by using foundation piles of different lengths with a system of beams; or, with a minimum of excavation, a platform capable of supporting a house can be built.

If the floor area cannot be enlarged by expanding the basic rectangular shape, other solutions are the L-shaped plan (fig. 25), where kitchen and utility rooms are placed in the angle between the sleeping and living rooms, and the T-shaped and the cruciform plans (fig. 26).

Projecting one of the façades to produce a T-shaped plan is particularly appropriate where the best view would otherwise be limited to the narrow end of the house. With this

12, 13. Even with this compact solution, dining area and seating area are separated from each other. The living room occupies more than half of the floor area. The island-type kitchen unit forms the centre (Page 18).

12, 13. Selbst bei dieser Kompaktlösung sind Eßplatz und Sitzgruppe voneinander getrennt. Der Wohnbereich nimmt über die Hälfte der Grundfläche ein. Der freistehende Küchenblock bildet das Zentrum (Seite 18).

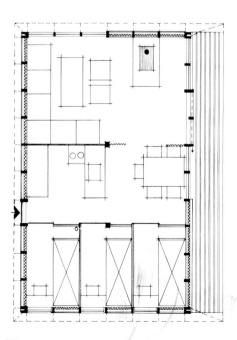

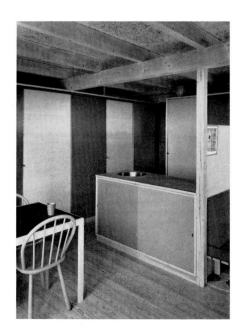

14, 15. Two kitchens as an integral part of the living room (Pages 141 and 158).

14, 15. Die Küche als integrierter Teil des Wohnraums (Seite 141 und 158).

solution, it is generally the living room and the master bedroom which are placed in the cross wings, since the angles between the wings are well suited to provide protected terraces and porches.

Houses built in a valley, in woods, or near water where there is a risk of flooding, are often mounted on stilts (fig. 27) so that they are not affected by soil humidity or ground water. Part of the space at ground level is often taken up by a walled unit containing service equipment such as heating installation or water pump. The remainder is left open to serve as a car port, a covered playground for the children, or, as in many examples, a sheltered sitting area with open fireplace or a shady retreat on a hot sunny day (fig. 28).

Another basic type, particularly popular in extreme climatic conditions in the high mountains or at the seaside, is derived from the shape of a tent. Apart from smaller and sometimes rather compact solutions with only one storey (fig. 29), many designs provide for a larger tent-type structure with a ridge sufficiently high to accommodate another bedroom on an upper floor (fig. 31). The sloping roofs generally extend down to ground level and are windowless (fig. 30); daylight enters through recessed, triangular all-glass gabled walls at the front and rear.

Often the upper storey does not extend over the entire ground floor area, but leaves the living room partly open to the roof. The remaining floor area is covered by the upper storey with bedrooms accessible from a gallery (fig. 32). In smaller houses of this type, the gallery floor is often separated from the living room merely by a balustrade. The feeling of spaciousness, however, is obtained at the cost of poor sound insulation between gallery, bedroom and living room.

Other compact plan types are based on the triangle, square (figs. 35, 36), pentagon, and hexagon (fig. 34). Solutions of this type, particularly popular for ski huts, have the advantage that all the rooms can be heated rapidly and evenly from a central source. And with these forms, too, the sense of space can be increased by providing porticoes or ring-shaped galleries. These precise geometric forms, which include even the classic pyramid, contrast with plans in which individual rooms are loosely linked together by passages and circulation lobbies (fig. 37). This approach may well gain in popularity through the use of pre-fabricated room units.

Given a temperate climate and appropriate services, there are few restrictions on architectural character. A steel framed cube with glass walls on all sides is as acceptable for holiday or vacation use as the virtually enclosed stone cube with small windows. Whether one favours an extrovert plan, with full-height glass walls open to the landscape (fig. 33), or a more closed design where family life is centered around a fire-side pit (fig. 34) and landscape is visible only through carefully dimensioned picture-like openings in the wall, is, after all, merely a matter of personal preference.

Many examples are designed to blend into the landscape, either in observance of building bye-laws or regulations for the protection of natural amenities, or in accordance with the owner's wishes. In the choice and treatment of materials attempts are often made to comply with local tradition. This applies particularly to houses erected in natural stone or timber by local craftsmen. Many of the examples in the present volume show that this method—which has the incidental advantage of being relatively cheap—need not lead to miniature peasant cottages in regional style. There are several dwellings

16. A practical ante-room where, during the winter, skis and clothing can be deposited. Wet ski boots can be left to dry on the bars below the bench. Dry clothing is kept in the wall cupboards on the left (Page 144).

16. Ein praktischer Vorraum, der im Winter als Ski- und Kleiderablage dient. Trockene Kleidung in den Wandschränken links; nasse Skistiefel trocknen auf den Stangen unter der Bank (Seite 144).

17, 18. Relationship between house type and climate: Protective rubble walling by the Mediterranean; timber construction and large windows on the sunny side of the Finnish house (Pages 70 and 78).

17, 18. Hausform und Klima: Schützende Steinmauern am Mittelmeer; wärmehaltende Holzbauweise und große Fenster auf der Sonnenseite in Finnland (Seite 70 und 78).

in which local tradition has been interpreted in a consistently modern sense with the aid of local materials.

In forest regions such as Finland, timber is the favourite material both for house construction and for furniture, since timber houses are not only relatively cheap to build but also to heat. Similarly, 'do it yourself' systems, where pre-fabricated units are delivered to the site ready for erection or for cutting to specification at the nearest saw mill, are nearly always made mostly of timber.

A number of special problems are discussed in the descriptions of individual houses—for example, burglar protection for the unoccupied house. Some interesting solutions to this problem are shown (figs. 38–42). Other designs are notable for the way room functions can be varied by such devices as moving partitions and tip-up beds. However, there seems to be some resistance to the idea of multi-purpose rooms and furniture. It is, after all, an important advantage of a comfortable vacation house that conversion from day-time to night-time use is unnecessary.

Although due regard has been given to structural details, the main purpose of this book is to clarify, by the comparison of successful examples, the problems of function and form that need to be taken into account in the design of a holiday or vacation house.

19. The large living room with materials easy to maintain: the ideal solution for the house of a large family (Page 86).

19. Der große Aufenthaltsraum mit leicht zu pflegenden Materialien: die Ideallösung für das Ferienhaus einer kinderreichen Familie (Seite 86).

Bei der Vielfalt an Möglichkeiten, die dieses Buch mit fünfzig internationalen Beispielen vor Augen führt, ist es nicht ganz einfach, das Ferienhaus von ähnlichen Bauaufgaben zu unterscheiden. An der Obergrenze gerät es in die Nachbarschaft des villenartigen Landhauses, das im Raumprogramm und Komfort völlig dem städtischen Einfamilienhaus gleicht. An der Untergrenze überschneidet es sich mit dem einfacher ausgestatteten Wochenendhaus. Am deutlichsten ist zweifellos die Unterscheidung gegenüber der primitiven, nur für vorübergehende Benutzung gedachten Notunterkunft, die als Jagdhütte oder Schrebergartenlaube lediglich Wetterschutz geben soll und meist ohne jeglichen architektonischen Anspruch erstellt wird.

Das Ferienhaus mit dem Campingzelt und dem Wohnwagenanhänger zu vergleichen, wie es immer wieder geschieht, verbietet sich eigentlich schon wegen der unterschiedlichen Kosten, vor allem aber wegen der Verschiedenartigkeit des Verwendungszwecks und der Ansprüche, die jeweils gestellt werden können. Die Wahl zwischen diesen drei Möglichkeiten einer Ferienunterkunft ist letzten Endes eine rein persönliche Entscheidung, und es wäre sinnlos, etwa die Mobilität von Zelt und Wohnwagen gegen die Ortsgebundenheit des Ferienhauses auszuspielen. Genau so gut könnte man gewichtige Argumente finden, die zugunsten des Ferienhauses sprechen. So ließe sich zum Beispiel darauf hinweisen, daß es dank seiner größeren Nutzfläche mehr Bewegungsfreiheit bietet und eine klare Trennung in Bereiche oder Räume für Wohnen und Schlafen erlaubt; daß die Installation von sanitären und haustechnischen Einrichtungen nur vom Geldbeutel und von den Komfortwünschen abhängt oder daß das Hausrecht auf eigenem Grund und Boden eindeutige Distanzverhältnisse zu eventuellen Nachbarn schafft.

Wie bei Zelt und Wohnwagen spielt sich auch beim Ferienhaus ein Gutteil aller Aktivität im Freien ab. Das »Outdoor Living« überwiegt normalerweise gegenüber dem Aufenthalt im Hausinneren. Der entscheidende Vorteil wird deshalb erst bei Regenwetter ganz deutlich, wenn sich das Leben für Stunden oder Tage ausschließlich ins Haus verlagert. Dann zeigt sich die Annehmlichkeit reichlichen Innenraums, womöglich mit der Aufteilung in mehrere Zimmer, die das Zusammenrücken auf engstem Raum erspart.

Deshalb geht die Tendenz heute mehr und mehr weg vom reinen »Dach über dem Kopf«, von der bloßen Schlafunterkunft, zu Lösungen, die genügend Spielraum für unterschiedliche »Indoor«-Beschäftigungen bieten. In diesem Sinne dürfte beispielsweise das japanische Kunststoff-Ei (Abb. 1–3) – bei allem Respekt vor der technischen Leistung in bezug auf Isolation, elektrische und sanitäre Ausstattung – allenfalls Minimalansprüchen an ein Ferienhaus genügen. Auf längere Zeit ist darin ein reibungsloses Zusammenleben nur bei weitgehend übereinstimmenden Lebensgewohnheiten und beträchtlicher Disziplin der Bewohner denkbar.

Kriterien wie der Spielraum an Bewegungsfreiheit oder das Maß der noch tragbar erscheinenden Provisorien helfen auch am ehesten, die fließenden Grenzen zwischen Ferienhaus und Wochenendhaus zu bestimmen. Was bei der Einzelübernachtung im Wochenendhaus als kurzweilige Abwechslung empfunden wird – das Wasserholen am Brunnen, die Petroleumbeleuchtung oder ein Speisezettel, dem man das Fehlen eines Kühlschranks anmerkt – das kann sich bei einem mehrwöchigen Aufenthalt als lästige Begleiterscheinung auswirken. Anders ausgedrückt: An die Ausstattung des Ferienhauses werden höhere Ansprüche gestellt, denn der Wunsch nach Ungebundenheit ist keineswegs gleichbedeutend mit dem Verzicht auf jeden Komfort. Weil sich diese Anschauung inzwischen auch bei den Erbauern von Wochenendhäusern durchgesetzt hat, sind die Unterschiede gegenüber dem Ferienhaus immer mehr im Schwinden. So ent-

20, 21. Relationship between house type and building density: Glass house in a park setting, open on all sides; enclosed walls of a 'castle' in a beach colony (Pages 58 and 126).

20, 21. Hausform und Bebauungsdichte: Allseitige Offenheit eines Glashauses im Parkgelände; ringsum geschlossene Wände einer »Burg« in einer Strandkolonie (Seite 58 und 126).

22. An example of the house type and plan most frequently encountered: oblong, single-storey building on a rectangular plan (Page 26).

22. Ein Beispiel für den häufigsten Haus- und Grundrißtyp: der langgestreckte, eingeschossige Baukörper mit rechteckigem Grundriß (Seite 26).

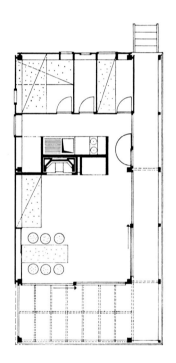

23. Standard plan of the rectangular type where kitchen and bathroom are placed between bedrooms and living room (Page 28).
24. On a sloping site, earthworks can be avoided by placing the house on a platform supported by posts of different length (Page 28).

23. Der Standardgrundriß des Rechtecktyps mit der Installationszelle zwischen Schlaf- und Wohnteil (Seite 28).
24. Bei abfallendem Grundstück erspart die Unterkonstruktion mit verschieden langen Pfosten das Planieren (Seite 28).

hält dieses Buch nur Lösungen, die sich ohne wesentliche Einschränkung für einen längeren Aufenthalt eignen.

Trotz aller Verschiedenartigkeit läßt sich durchaus ein gemeinsamer Nenner für die folgenden Beispiele finden: Sie bilden den architektonischen Rahmen für eine Lebensweise, die mehr oder weniger mit der Alltagsexistenz des Stadtmenschen kontrastiert. Die wesentlichsten Merkmale dieses »Ausnahmezustandes« sind die enge Verbundenheit mit der Natur und die Zwanglosigkeit der Lebensumstände. Die Ungebundenheit äußert sich nicht nur im erholsamen Rhythmuswechsel gegenüber dem Alltag, sondern auch in der betont informellen Haltung, mit der man von den gewohnten Konventionen abrückt. Eine solche Einstellung ist jedoch keineswegs gleichbedeutend mit der sentimentalen Attitüde des »Zurück-zum-einfachen-Leben«.

Besondere Aktualität gewinnt das Ferienhaus für Familien mit Kindern, die sich nicht dem Reglement einer Hotel-Hausordnung unterwerfen möchten, aber auch dem Campingplatz nichts abzugewinnen vermögen. Ihnen bietet es das ideale Ferienmilieu, das einerseits jeder persönlichen Stimmung und nahezu jedem Hobby Raum läßt, aber doch auch ein intensiveres Zusammenleben ermöglicht als der Alltag mit Beruf und Schule.

Aus diesen Faktoren, zu denen auch noch das Problem des Personalmangels zu rechnen ist, ergeben sich ganz bestimmte Konsequenzen für die Planung eines Ferienhauses. Es sollte ein möglichst freizügiges Überwechseln von drinnen nach draußen gestatten (Abb. 4+5), mit ausreichenden Verbindungen zum Freiraum und mit den verschiedensten Typen von ganz oder teilweise überdeckten Freisitzplätzen (Abb. 6–10), die als

Loggien, Balkone, Terrassen oder Pergolen den engeren Hausbereich ergänzen und den nötigen Sonnen- oder Windschutz geben. Bei der Grundrißdisposition ist ein großer Aufenthaltsraum vorzusehen (Abb. 19) und zumindest für Eßplatz und Sitzgruppe verschiedene Bereiche einzurichten (Abb. 12 + 13). Die Großzügigkeit bei der Bemessung des Tagesraumes sollte jedoch nicht zu stark auf Kosten der Schlafräume gehen, damit diese auch tagsüber einmal die Möglichkeit zum Sichzurückziehen bieten. Es empfiehlt sich, den Schlafbereich von Kindern durch hinreichende Schalldämmung abzuschirmen oder ihn so zu legen, daß die Erwachsenen am Abend nicht nur im Flüsterton miteinander sprechen können. Bei größeren Ferienhäusern, die auch Gastfamilien aufnehmen sollen, wird man versuchen, die Gästeräume in einem besonderen Flügel oder Geschoß zusammenzufassen. Einige Aufmerksamkeit verdient auch die Anordnung des Küchenbereiches. Selbst in den Fällen, in denen er nicht nur aus einer Kochnische (Abb. 11) oder aus einem frei im Raum stehenden Küchenblock (Abb. 13) mit Herd, Arbeitsfläche und Spüle besteht, wird die Küche nur selten völlig vom Wohnraum abgetrennt, denn damit würde man ja auch die Hausfrau vom Familiengeschehen isolieren. Vor allem unter den amerikanischen Beispielen dominieren die Lösungen, bei denen die Küchenelemente offen im Wohnraum stehen oder an einer Wand entlang aufgereiht sind (Abb. 14). Sehr bewährt haben sich, besonders bei Ferienhäusern in Wintersportgebieten, Vorräume am Hauseingang (Abb. 16), die als Skiablage und als Trockenraum für nasse Überkleidung dienen; aber auch Sportgeräte, Angelzeug oder Gummistiefel finden dort einen guten Platz. – Und nicht zuletzt sollte die Überlegung, die Hausfrau in den Ferien so weit als irgend möglich von der Hausarbeit zu entlasten, bei der Planung berücksichtigt werden. Ein vernünftiger Grundriß, der überflüssige Wege und unnötigen Kräfteaufwand erspart, kann ihr ebenso das Leben erleichtern wie die Auswahl von Materialien, die sich leicht pflegen lassen. Ein Ferienhaus in den Dünen, wo ständig Sand ins Innere getragen wird, mit Teppichen auszulegen, wäre ebenso unsinnig wie ein Parkettfußboden in der Skihütte.

Natürlich erfahren Entwurfsregeln dieser Art von Land zu Land und von Region zu Region ihre Abwandlungen. So haben spanische und lateinamerikanische Ferienhäuser oft mehrere Dienstbotenzimmer oder einen regelrechten Dienstbotenflügel, weil das Personal auch in der Ferienzeit zur Verfügung steht. Umgekehrt scheinen sich Architekten und Bauherren in den USA am meisten darüber Gedanken zu machen, wie sich die Hausarbeit im Ferienhaus auf ein Minimum beschränken läßt. Eine entsprechende technische Ausstattung mit Kühlschrank, Waschmaschine und anderen elektrischen Haushaltsgeräten gehört daher zu den Selbstverständlichkeiten. Ein Haus am Mittelmeer wird sich durch massive Stein- oder Betonwände am ehesten vor der Hitze schützen lassen (Abb. 17), während es beim finnischen Holzhaus nur willkommen ist, wenn die Sonne die Fensterflächen aufheizt (Abb. 18). Daß die Luvseite eines Strandhauses mit Windschutzmauern abgeschirmt werden sollte, versteht sich ebenso von selbst wie die schneesichere Dachausbildung bei einem Ferienhaus im Hochgebirge. Auch zwischen der Bebauungsdichte und der Hausform besteht eine Wechselbeziehung. Auf einem mehrere Hektar großen Areal läßt sich ein Ferienhaus nach allen Seiten öffnen (Abb. 20), hingegen zwingt eine schmale Parzelle in dicht besiedelten Feriengebieten wie Long Island zu einem mehr introvertierten Plan (Abb. 21). Dabei ist es oft nicht einfach, den Wunsch

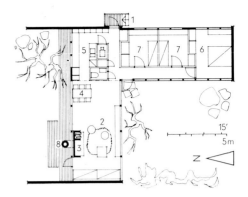

25. L-shaped plan as an extension of the rectangular plan. Key: 1 Entrance, 2 Living room, 3 Fireplace, 4 Dining area, 5 Kitchen, 6 Master bedroom, 7 Children's room, 8 Terrace (Page 80).

25. Die L-Form als Erweiterung des Rechteckgrundrisses. Legende: 1 Eingang, 2 Wohnraum, 3 Kamin, 4 Eßplatz, 5 Küche, 6 Eltern, 7 Kinder, 8 Terrasse (Seite 80).

26. Cruciform plan where the bedrooms are placed in the cross wings (Page 99).
27, 28. Rectangular house placed on stilts, where parts of the open ground floor are used as a car port or terrace (Pages 89 and 92).

26. Kreuzförmiger Grundriß mit Schlafräumen in den Querflügeln (Seite 99).
27, 28. Das auf Stützen gestellte Rechteckhaus (Seite 89 und 92).

nach Spielfläche und Sitzplätzen im Freien mit dem Bestreben zu vereinen, sich gegen Einblick von den Nachbargrundstücken abzuschirmen.

Trotz solcher Einschränkungen lassen sich unter den Beispielen dieses Bandes gewisse Grundtypen in Hausform und Grundrißlösung feststellen, die durchaus miteinander vergleichbar sind. Am häufigsten ist der Typ einer eingeschossigen rechteckigen »Schachtel« (Abb. 22), deren Grundriß in zwei Hälften unterteilt wurde (Abb. 23), wobei die eine Hälfte die Schlafräume aufnimmt, während in der anderen der Wohnbereich und oft auch eine überdeckte Terrasse untergebracht sind. Die Nahtstelle zwischen den beiden Hausteilen wird durch die Installationszelle mit WC, Bad oder Duschraum und Küchenbereich markiert. Zumindest auf der Sonnen- und Wetterseite kragt im allgemeinen das Dach, das meist als Flachdach ausgeführt ist, so weit aus, daß es Fenster und Freisitzplatz vor steiler Sonne und Schlagregen schützt. Dieser Grundtyp, der mit einfachen Streifen- oder Pfahlfundamenten auskommt, ist ebenso wirtschaftlich wie variabel. Liegt das Grundstück am Hang (Abb. 24), so läßt sich der nötige Niveauausgleich durch verschieden lange Fundamentpfähle erreichen und bei einem Minimum an Erdbewegungen ein tragfähiger Balkenrost oder eine Plattform für den Hauskörper schaffen.

Soll die Nutzfläche vergrößert werden und reicht dafür eine entsprechende Ausdehnung der reinen Rechteckform allein nicht aus, so bieten sich verschiedene Möglichkeiten für die Bereicherung des Grundrisses. Am häufigsten sind die L-Form (Abb. 25) – bei der die Wirtschaftsräume am Knick liegen und Schlafen und Wohnen auf die beiden Flügel verteilt ist – und die T-Form mit der Variante des kreuzförmigen Grundrisses (Abb. 26). Die Verbreiterung einer Stirnfront beim T-Grundriß empfiehlt sich vor allem dort, wo ein Haus sonst nur mit der Schmalseite zur schönsten Aussicht hin orientiert werden könnte. Meist sind bei dieser Lösung in den Querarmen die Wohnräume oder auch der Elternschlafraum untergebracht, und die Winkel zwischen den Flügeln eignen sich besonders gut für geschützte Terrassen und Freisitzplätze.

In Talmulden, in Waldgebieten oder auch in Wassernähe, wo mit Überschwemmungsgefahr zu rechnen ist, werden alle diese Haustypen häufig auf Stützen gestellt (Abb. 27), so daß ihnen die Bodenfeuchtigkeit und das Grundwasser nichts anhaben können. Unter das Wohngeschoß schiebt sich dann zumeist ein fest ummauerter Sockelkern, der technische Einrichtungen wie Heizung oder Wasserpumpe aufnimmt; der übrige Raum zwischen den Stützen bleibt frei und dient zum Unterstellen des Wagens oder als regensicherer Kinderspielplatz. Oft wird der offene Stützenbereich auch als überdeckter Sitzplatz benutzt, und an heißen Tagen ist er als Schattenzone beliebt (Abb. 28).

Ein anderer Grundtypus, der sich speziell unter extremen klimatischen Bedingungen im Hochgebirge oder auch an der See bewährt, geht von der Zeltform aus. Neben kleineren, teilweise sehr kompakten Lösungen (Abb. 29), die nur ein Stockwerk aufweisen, finden sich häufig Entwürfe auf vergrößerter Grundfläche, bei denen der First so hoch liegt, daß ein zusätzliches Schlafgeschoß eingebaut werden kann (Abb. 31). Die beiden seitlichen Dachflächen sind meist bis zur Erde heruntergezogen und die Dachschrägen geschlossen gehalten (Abb. 30); die Belichtung erfolgt über das zurückgesetzte, manchmal ganz in Glas aufgelöste Dreieck der Vorder- und Rückfront. Oft geht das zusätzlich eingezogene Geschoß nicht durch die volle Tiefe des Hauses, so daß sich ein zweigeschossiger Wohnteil ergibt, der bis zum Dachfirst hinaufreicht, und eine Galerie mit Schlafräumen

29, 30. Tent-shaped houses: Prefabricated miniature variant, and three-storey tent house (Pages 130 and 132).

31. Bedroom under the roof ridge of a tent house (Page 132).

32. Tent house with living room extending to the roof ridge, and open bedroom gallery (Page 134).

29, 30. Zeltformen: die vorfabrizierte Minimumlösung und das dreigeschossige Zelthaus (Seite 130 und 132).

31. Schlafraum unter dem First eines Zelthauses (Seite 132).

32. Zelthaus mit firsthohem Wohnteil und offener Schlafgalerie (Seite 134).

33, 34. Contrast between 'extrovert' and 'introvert' plans (Pages 58 and 141).

33, 34. Nach außen orientierte Raumgruppierung und zentrierte Bauweise (Seite 58 und 141).

(Abb. 32). Bei kleineren Lösungen dieser Art beschränkt man sich gern darauf, das Galeriegeschoß zum Wohnraum hin nur durch eine Brüstung zu begrenzen. Der Vorteil der großzügigeren Raumwirkung bringt dann allerdings den Nachteil mit sich, daß die Schlafgalerie akustisch nur ungenügend zum Wohnraum hin abgeschirmt ist.

Andere kompakte Hausformen bauen auf Zentralgrundrissen auf, die vom Dreieck, Quadrat (Abb. 35 + 36), Fünf- oder Sechseck (Abb. 34) ausgehen. Lösungen dieser Art, die sich vor allem bei Skihütten finden, haben den Vorteil, daß alle Räume von einer zentralen Heizquelle aus verhältnismäßig rasch und gleichmäßig erwärmt werden können. Durch den Einbau von Umgängen und ringförmigen Galerien läßt sich auch bei diesen Entwürfen der Raumeindruck steigern. Im Gegensatz zu solchen polygonalen und stereometrischen Hausformen, die bis zur klassischen Pyramide reichen (Abb. 36), stehen schließlich jene Lösungen, bei denen sich einzelne Raumzellen verselbständigen und nur noch locker durch Gänge oder Verteilerräume miteinander verbunden werden (Abb. 37). Es wäre denkbar, daß sich dieses System durch die Verwendung präfabrizierter Raumzellen noch weiterentwickeln ließe.

Von der formalen Seite her gibt es für die architektonische Gestaltung so gut wie keine Einschränkungen. Unter bestimmten klimatischen Bedingungen oder bei entsprechend aufwendiger technischer Installation ist der rundum verglaste Kubus mit Stahlskelett genauso möglich wie der geschlossene Steinwürfel mit kleinen Fensterluken. Ob man sein Haus durch raumhohe Glaswände in die Landschaft hinaus orientiert (Abb. 33) oder ob man es mehr auf seinen eigenen Mittelpunkt, etwa einen allseits freistehenden Kamin mit dazugehöriger Sitzgrube (Abb. 34), bezieht und die Natur lediglich durch sorgfältig bemessene, bilderähnliche Wandausschnitte genießen möchte, ist letzten Endes nur eine Frage der persönlichen Entscheidung.

Durch Zwang von außen – in Form von Bauvorschriften oder Bestimmungen des Landschaftsschutzes –, oft aber auch auf Wunsch des Bauherrn fügen sich viele Ferienhäuser unauffällig in die Landschaft ein. Auch in der Materialwahl und in der Verarbeitung wird nicht selten versucht, sich an die lokale Tradition anzupassen. Das gilt ganz besonders für Ferienhäuser, die von einheimischen Handwerkern in Naturstein oder Holz errichtet werden. Daß dieses Verfahren, das zudem noch den Vorteil hat, verhältnismäßig billig zu sein, nicht zwangsläufig zu Miniatur-Bauernhäusern im Heimatstil führen muß, wird an einer ganzen Reihe von Beispielen dieses Buches deutlich, bei denen mit bodenständigem Material Lösungen geschaffen wurden, die die Tradition in einem konsequent modernen Sinne interpretieren. In waldreichen Gebieten wie etwa Finnland ist Holz das bevorzugte Material für Konstruktion und Innenausbau, denn Holzhäuser lassen sich in diesen Gegenden nicht nur mit relativ geringen Kosten erstellen, sondern auch mit wenig Aufwand beheizen. Montagesysteme für den Selbstbau, bei denen die Bauteile vom Verkäufer fertig angeliefert oder nach einer Stückliste im nächsten Sägewerk zugeschnitten werden, basieren gleichfalls fast immer auf Holzkonstruktionen.

35, 36. Four-gable house with folding roof, and pyramid-shaped house (Pages 138 and 136).
37. Cellular room units arranged informally in a fan pattern and linked by passageways (Page 122).

35, 36. Vier-Giebel-Haus mit Faltdach und Pyramidenhaus (Seite 138 und 136).
37. Durch Gänge verbundene Raumzellen in lockerem Fächergrundriß (Seite 122).

Auf eine Reihe von Spezialproblemen wird bei der Dokumentation der einzelnen Beispiele näher eingegangen, so vor allem auf die Sicherung des unbewohnten Hauses gegen Einbruch, deren interessanteste Lösungen in den Abbildungen 38–42 vorweggenommen sind. Andere Entwürfe geben bemerkenswerte Anregungen für die Wandelbarkeit der Raumfunktion mit Hilfe von Faltwänden und Klappbetten, wenn sich auch im allgemeinen eher eine gewisse Zurückhaltung gegenüber der Konvertibilität von Raum und Mobiliar beobachten läßt. Schließlich ist es gerade ein wesentlicher Vorteil des Ferienhauses, die Verwandlung in Tag- und Nachtstellung überflüssig zu machen. Bei aller Bedeutung, die dem konstruktiven Detail zugemessen wurde, entstand dieses Buch jedoch vorwiegend aus der Absicht, durch die Zusammenstellung bemerkenswerter Beispiele zur Klärung der allgemeinen funktionalen und formalen Probleme beizutragen, die beim Bau eines Ferienhauses beachtet werden sollten.

38–42. Examples of burglary protection by shutters. Figs. 38, 39: The terrace in front of the house has a number of individual panels which can, for protection purposes, be tilted up and fixed by bolts from inside (Page 21). Figs. 40, 41: Hardboard panels, suspended from rails, can be pushed sideways in front of a windowless panel (Page 32). Fig. 42: Shutters can be tilted up by 90° and fastened to a cross beam (Page 54).

38–42. Beispiele für die Einbruchsicherung durch Läden. Abb. 38, 39: Die Terrasse vor dem Haus ist in einzelne Felder unterteilt, die zum Schutz hochgeklappt und mit Bolzen von innen verschraubt werden können (Seite 21). Abb. 40, 41: Schiebewände aus Hartfaserplatten, die oben in Schienen laufen, werden beim Öffnen vor ein fest verschaltes Wandstück geschoben (Seite 32). Abb. 42: Klappläden werden um 90° nach oben geschwenkt und an einem Überzug befestigt (Seite 54).

Weekend house near Aarhus

Architect: Hans Peder Sølvsten, Højbjerg
Interior designer: Harbo Sølvsten, Aarhus

This house, covering an area of not more than 400 sq ft, stands on a hill near the coast south of Aarhus. By resorting to simple design and inexpensive materials, it was possible to keep the cost low. The wooden structure, covering an area of 7.81 × 4.84 m, conforms to a module of 75.5 × 75.5 cm. On the outside, the house is covered with dark-stained deal boards. The same material, though untreated, has also been used indoors. Insulation consists of woodwool cement slabs which remain visible at the ceiling. This insulation is so effective that the house can also be used throughout the winter. With its skilfully designed layout and compact furnishing, the interior gives the appearance of being more spacious than it really is.

Wochenendhaus bei Aarhus

Architekt: Hans Peder Sølvsten, Højbjerg
Inneneinrichtung: Harbo Sølvsten, Aarhus

Dieses Wochenendhaus, das eine Fläche von nur 38 m² überdeckt, liegt südlich von Aarhus auf einem Hügel nahe der Küste. Durch die einfache Konstruktion und die Verwendung billiger Baustoffe war es möglich, die Baukosten niedrig zu halten. Auf einer Grundfläche von 7,81 × 4,84 m wurde eine Holzkonstruktion errichtet, der ein Rastermaß von 75,5 × 75,5 cm zugrunde liegt. Das Gebäude ist außen mit dunkelgebeizten Dielenbrettern verschalt. Für die Verschalung der Innenräume sind ebenfalls Kiefernbretter verwendet, die jedoch roh belassen wurden. Zur Isolierung sind Holzfaser-Zementplatten benutzt, die an der Decke unverputzt sichtbar bleiben. Diese Isolierung ist so wirkungsvoll, daß das Haus auch im Winter benutzt werden kann. Durch geschickte Grundrißdisposition und kompakte Möblierung wirkt der Innenraum wesentlich geräumiger als er in Wirklichkeit ist.

1. The south side with the overhanging roof.

2. Plan. Key: 1 Sitting room, 2 Fireplace, 3 Dining area, 4 Kitchen, 5 Sleeping bunks, 6 Veranda.

3. The window-less northside with the two-part entrance door.

4. Foundation plan. The wooden structure stands on concrete piers measuring 20×20×100 cm.

5. Fireplace, seen from the dining area. The exit to the veranda on the right can be closed by a sliding door. The service counter from the kitchen, on the left, can be curtained off by a wooden shutter.

6. Cross-section. The height, measured to the bottom edge of the ceiling joists, is 2.18 metres (7 ft 2 in).

7. Chairs and table in the sitting room. The low screen (6 ft) between this corner and the kitchen has a raffia cloth cladding.

1. Blick auf die Südseite, deren Podest vom Dachüberstand beschattet wird.

2. Grundriß: 1 Wohnraum, 2 Kaminofen, 3 Eßplatz, 4 Küche, 5 Schlafkojen, 6 Veranda.

3. Ansicht der fensterlosen Nordseite mit der zweiteiligen Eingangstür.

4. Fundamentplan. Die Holzkonstruktion ruht auf Betonpfeilern von 20×20×100 cm.

5. Blick vom Eßplatz zum Kaminofen. Der Austritt zur Veranda rechts kann durch eine Schiebetür geschlossen werden. Ganz links ist über der Anrichte des Küchenteils ein Rollo aus Holzstabgewebe zu erkennen.

6. Querschnitt. Die Raumhöhe bis zur Unterkante der Deckenbalken beträgt 2,18 m.

7. Sitzgruppe im Wohnraum mit Blick auf das Meer. Die 1,8 m hohe Trennwand zwischen der Wohnecke und der Küche ist mit Bastgeflecht verkleidet.

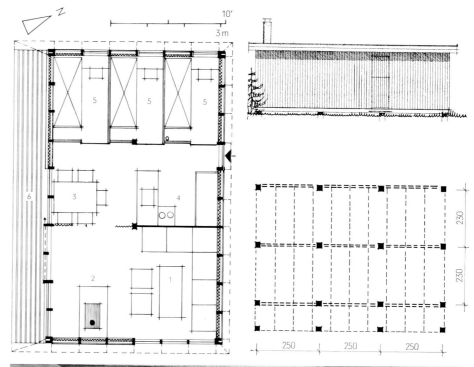

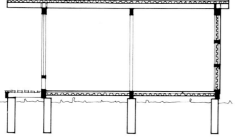

8. One of the three sleeping berths. Each of them covers an area of 3×2 module squares. The upper bunks in each room are only used as spare beds. Next to each of the 75.5 cm wide beds is a table top, mounted on brackets.

9. View from the dining area to the two-part entrance door. The upper wing can be opened separately to improve lighting and ventilation. On the right are the service counter and kitchen cupboard.

10. Dining area and kitchen seen from the sitting room. The three sliding doors leading to the bedrooms have a coat of coloured varnish; the walls between the doors are cloth covered. Between the joists, the untreated woodwool cement boards remain visible.

8. Eine der drei knapp bemessenen Schlafkojen, die alle gleiche Ausmaße haben (226,5 × 151 cm = 3 × 2 Rasterfelder). Die oberen der Doppelstockbetten werden nur als Notlager benutzt. Neben jedem der 75,5 cm breiten Betten ist auf Konsolen eine Tischplatte befestigt.

9. Blick vom Eßplatz auf die zweigeteilte Eingangstür, deren Flügel zur Belichtung und Belüftung aufgeklappt werden kann. Rechts Anrichte und Küchenschrank.

10. Blick aus dem Wohnteil auf Eßplatz und Küche. Die drei Schiebetüren zu den Schlafkojen sind farbig lackiert, die Wandflächen zwischen den Türen tragen textile Bespannung. Zwischen den Deckenbalken sind die roh belassenen Holzfaser-Zementplatten zu erkennen.

Cottage near Krefeld

Architect: Ernst Althoff, Krefeld
Associate: H. van Schayck

This wooden cottage conforms to the strict German building regulations by which the size of such a cottage is limited to a maximum of 30 sq metres, plus 10 sq. metres for a terrace. The design is deliberately based on the use of the simplest manually or industrially produced components so that the cottage can be assembled even by laymen without special tools. The wooden platform serving as terrace consists of separate panels which can be tilted up to form window shutters. A small entrance hall leads, on the left, to the living room with dining area and kitchenette. The bedroom is to the right of the core which consists of kitchenette, a small bathroom, and WC. The front of the house is entirely of glass, with the posts serving as window frames. A connection to the electricity supply is provided.

Ferienhaus bei Krefeld

Architekt: Ernst Althoff, Krefeld
Mitarbeiter: H. van Schayck

Das Holzhaus entspricht den in Deutschland streng gehandhabten baupolizeilichen Vorschriften, die die Größe einer Wohnlaube auf maximal 30 m² + 10 m² Terrasse beschränken. Der Entwurf ist auf einfachste handwerkliche oder industriell herstellbare Details abgestimmt, so daß er auch von Nichtfachleuten ohne Spezialgeräte realisiert werden kann. Über die Terrasse, die in mehreren Teilen als Schutz gegen die Fensterfront geklappt werden kann, erreicht man eine kleine Diele, an die sich links der Wohnraum mit Eßplatz und Kochnische anschließt. Der Schlafraum liegt rechts von der Installationszelle, die aus Kochnische und Kleinbad mit WC gebildet wird. Die Frontseite ist ganz in Glas aufgelöst, wobei die Verglasung fest zwischen die Pfosten eingespannt wird. Für die Energieversorgung ist ein Anschluß an das Stromnetz vorgesehen.

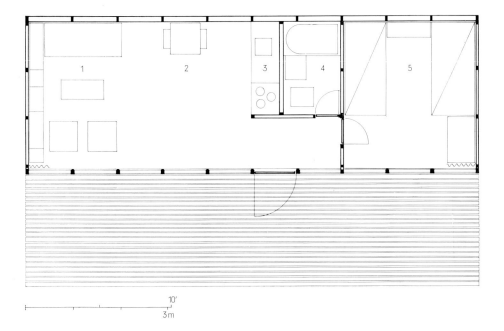

```
    1        2        3    4        5
```

10'
3m

1. (Page 21) The glass frontage with the platform panels dropped down.

2. (Page 21) Frontage with the platform panels partly drawn up to form window shutters.

3. Plan. Key: 1 Sitting area, 2 Dining area, 3 Kitchenette, 4 Bathroom and WC, 5 Bedroom. The plan can be varied, eg, by reducing the bedroom to two modular units (size of one unit: 0.95×3.25 metres) in which case the second bed would have to be placed above the other. The size can be reduced by a further modular unit by reducing the length of the sitting room from 5 to 4 units. The two additional units thus available can be used for the provision of a second sleeping berth, connected to the sitting room.

4. View from the sitting area across the dining area to the kitchenette; on the right is the entrance and, beyond it, the passage to the bedroom. Built in between the ceiling joists, the roofing and the large fixed windows are metal-framed ventilating windows.

5. Sitting room, seen from the entrance hall. In the foreground on the right is the dining area, in the background the sitting area, where the divan can be used as a spare bed. The inner walls are covered by vertically-hung spruce boards, left in natural colour.

1. (Seite 21) Die verglaste Frontseite mit heruntergeklappter Terrasse.

2. (Seite 21) Vorderfront mit teilweise hochgeklappter Terrasse.

3. Grundriß. Legende: 1 Wohnbereich, 2 Eßplatz, 3 Kochnische, 4 Bad und WC, 5 Schlafraum. Grundrißvarianten sehen unter anderem eine Verkleinerung des Schlafraums auf zwei Rasterfelder (Größe eines Feldes: 0,95×3,25 m) vor, wobei die beiden Betten übereinandergestellt werden müßten. Ein weiteres Feld läßt sich durch die Reduzierung des Wohnraums von fünf auf vier Achsen gewinnen. Die beiden zusätzlichen Felder, die sich auf diese Weise ergeben, lassen sich für den Einbau einer zweiten Schlafkoje im Anschluß an den Wohnraum verwenden.

4. Blick vom Wohnbereich über den Eßplatz auf die Kochnische, rechts daneben die Diele, dahinter der Durchgang zum Schlafraum. Zwischen den Deckenbalken, der Dachschalung und dem Rahmenwerk der großen, festverglasten Fenster sind verglaste Lüftungsflügel mit Metallrahmen eingebaut.

5. Blick aus der Diele in den Wohnraum. Rechts vorn der Eßplatz, im Hintergrund die Sitzgruppe, deren Couch als weitere Schlafgelegenheit benutzt werden kann. Die Innenräume sind mit naturfarbenen Tannenholzbrettern vertikal verschalt.

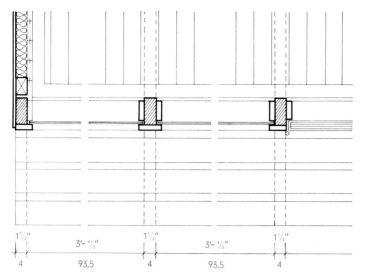

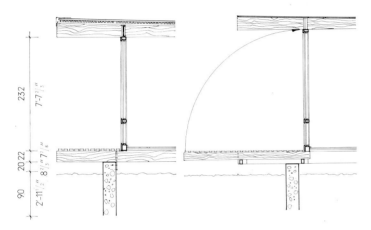

Construction: Two concrete strip foundations carry, at 95 cm centres, joists measuring 4×26×450 cm which are held by steel anchors embedded in the foundations. Nailed on these joists are 3 cm thick boards which are covered by plastic skin as a protection against rising damp and by a 1.5 cm thick Styropor panel for thermal insulation. Laths placed between these panels support the 2 cm thick tongued-and-grooved floor boarding. Inside the house, all these panels are covered with tongued-and-grooved boards. The outer walls are faced with asbestos cement panels insulated with foam plastic. (The special sheeting used on the outside is 8 mm thick).

The roof structure likewise consists of joists of 4×26×450 cm tapered to 15 cm at one end. These joists are supported by the timber posts to which they are firmly fastened. Nailed to these joists are 2.5 cm thick tongued-and-grooved boards which carry 2.0 cm thick panels of foamed plastic. These are, in their turn, covered by plastic skin and, finally, by the corrugated asbestos cement roofing.

Konstruktion: Auf zwei Streifenfundamenten aus Beton wird alle 95 cm eine Bohle 4×26×450 cm gelegt. Diese Bohlen werden an Stahlankern befestigt, die in das Fundament eingelassen sind. Auf die Bohlen wird eine 3 cm starke Schalung genagelt. Auf diese wird zum Schutz gegen von unten aufsteigende Feuchtigkeit eine Kunststoffolie gelegt. Hierauf kommt zur Wärmedämmung eine 1,5 cm starke Styroporplatte. Zwischen den Schaumstoffplatten liegen Leisten, die den 2 cm starken Fußboden aus Nut- und Federbrettern aufnehmen. Im Inneren des Hauses sind diese Rahmen alle mit Nut- und Federbrettern verschalt. Die Außenwände haben Schaumstoffplatten als Wärmedämmung und außen eine Verkleidung aus Asbestzementplatten. (Spezialplatten 8 mm stark.) Die Dachkonstruktion besteht ebenfalls aus 4×26×450 cm starken Bohlen, die sich an einem Ende auf 15 cm verjüngen. Die Bohlen ruhen auf den Pfosten des Rahmensystems und sind mit diesen fest verbunden. Auf die Dachbohlen wird eine 2,5 cm starke Nut- und Federschalung genagelt. Auf die Schalung wird eine 2,0 cm starke Schaumstoffplatte gelegt, die wieder mit einer Kunststoffolie abgedeckt wird. Hierauf liegt dann die Dacheindeckung aus Wellasbestzementplatten.

6. Plan of a corner of the house. The outer wall is faced with 6–8 mm thick asbestos cement panels; the walls between the posts have a Styropor filling. On the inside, the wall has a cladding of tongued-and-grooved spruce boards.
7. Cross-section of house front. Fixed windows, and metal-framed ventilating windows on top.
8. Cross-section of house front where the platform panels can be drawn up to serve as window shutters.
9. Detail of front wall. 1 Joists, 2 30 mm thick boarding, 3 15 mm thick Styropor panel, 4 Tongued-and-grooved floor boards, 5 Plinth, 6 Toplight with metal-framed ventilating window, 7 Roof joists, 8 Ceiling boards, 9 Styropor insulation, 10 Roofing of corrugated asbestos cement boards.

6. Grundriß einer Hausecke. Die Außenwand besteht aus einer 6–8 mm starken Verkleidung aus Asbestzementplatten, die Zwischenwände des Rahmenwerks mit Styropor ausgefüllt. Innenraumverkleidung mit Nut- und Federbrettern aus Tannenholz.
7. Schnitt durch die Frontseite. Glaswand mit fester Verglasung, Oberlichter als Klappflügel in Metallrahmen.
8. Schnitt durch die Frontseite. Variante mit Klappterrasse.
9. Detail der Wandkonstruktion an der Frontseite. Legende: 1 Binder, 2 Schalung 30 mm stark, 3 Styropor 15 mm stark, 4 Fußboden aus Nut- und Federbrettern, 5 Sockel, 6 Oberlicht mit Lüftungsflügel in Metallrahmen, 7 Binderbalken, 8 Deckenschalung, 9 Dämmschicht aus Styropor, 10 Dacheindeckung aus Wellasbestzementplatten.

23

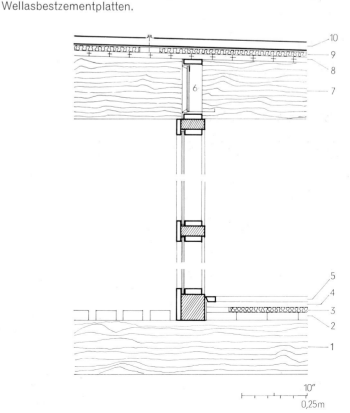

Cottage at Villinki, Finland

Architect: Osmo Sipari, Helsinki

This unpretentious cottage, unobtrusively merged with its surroundings, stands on the wooded and rocky shore of a Finnish lake. Its timber structure, faced externally and internally with raw deal boards, stands on the rubble wall foundation of a house destroyed by fire. The nearly square plan is so designed that dining area and kitchen face the morning sun in the east. The living room corner on the west side faces the lake. On the south side, a narrow, covered balcony forms the extension of the dining area. Another covered terrace is outside the guest room at the north-west corner. In the northern part of the house are all the bedrooms; the parents' bedroom in the north-eastern corner is merely separated from the children's beds by a short partition, no longer than the beds. The fireplace forms the centre of the house.

Ferienhaus in Villinki, Finnland

Architekt: Osmo Sipari, Helsinki

Das schlichte Ferienhaus, das sich unauffällig in seine Umgebung einfügt, steht am felsigen Ufer eines finnischen Waldsees. Sein außen und innen mit sägerauhen Tannenbrettern verschaltes Holzgerüst ruht auf dem Bruchsteinsockel eines abgebrannten Hauses. Der nahezu quadratische Grundriß ist so angelegt, daß Eßplatz und Küchenteil nach Osten in der Morgensonne liegen. Die auf der Westseite des Wohnraums eingerichtete Wohnecke hat Aussicht auf den See. Nach Süden bildet ein schmaler, gedeckter Balkon die Fortsetzung des Eßbereichs. Auch dem Gästezimmer an der Nordwestecke ist eine gedeckte Terrasse vorgelagert. Die nördliche Hälfte des Hauses nimmt sämtliche Schlafräume auf, wobei das Elternschlafzimmer von den Betten der Kinder nur durch eine Zwischenwand in Bettlänge getrennt ist. Der Kaminblock bildet das Zentrum des Hauses.

24

1. West side, with the large, slightly projecting living room and the guest room.
2. North side, with the terrace outside the guest room. The two windows belong to the bedroom for parents and children.
3. View from the living room corner towards the white-washed fireplace and the dining corner.
4. Plan. Key: 1 Entrance, 2 Covered terrace, 3 Guest room, 4 Bedroom, 5 Living room, 6 Fireplace, 7 Kitchen, 8 Dining corner, 9 Covered south balcony.
5. Living room corner, facing the lake, with the south balcony.

1. Die Westseite mit dem großen, etwas vorspringenden Wohnteil und dem Gästezimmer.
2. Ansicht von Norden mit der Terrasse vor dem Gästezimmer. Die beiden Fenster gehören zu dem Schlafraum für Eltern und Kinder.
3. Blick vom Wohnteil auf den weiß getünchten Kaminblock und die Eßecke.
4. Grundriß. Legende: 1 Eingang, 2 gedeckte Terrasse, 3 Gästezimmer, 4 Schlafraum, 5 Wohnbereich, 6 Kaminblock, 7 Küche, 8 Eßecke, 9 gedeckter Südbalkon.
5. Die Wohnecke mit Aussicht auf den See und den Südbalkon.

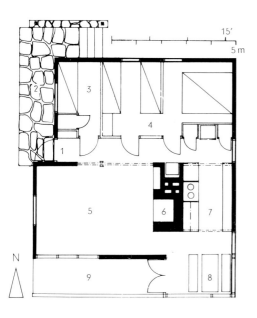

Weekend house in the Swabian Mountains

Architect: Fred Hochstrasser, Ulm and Winterthur

This weekend house for three adults has been erected in a large orchard on the southern slope of the Harthausen Valley near Ulm. Its basement is used for fruit storage. The net floor area was restricted by the bye-laws to 24 sq metres. The floor slab above the concrete basement projects as a platform, supported on the valley side by two steel columns. On the west side of the sitting-cum-bedroom, where the full-height double-glazed windows afford a view across the meadows and fields, is a bath room with shower bath and WC, and on the north side a covered stairway coming up from the basement. On the south side is the open veranda. The roof structure, freely supported by steel columns, consists of double-boarding with built-up roof. Outside as well as inside, the walls are faced with vertical wooden boards. The flooring consists of floor bricks.

Wochenendhaus auf der Schwäbischen Alb

Architekt: Fred Hochstrasser, Ulm und Winterthur

Dieses Wochenendhaus für drei Erwachsene wurde auf einer großen Obstwiese am Südhang des Harthauser Tals bei Ulm errichtet und dient zugleich als Obstlagerkeller. Laut baupolizeilicher Vorschrift durfte die Nettogrundfläche dabei nicht größer als 24 m² sein. Die Decke über dem betonierten Keller kragt als Plattform aus und ruht auf der Hangseite auf zwei Stahlstützen. An den Aufenthalts- und Schlafraum, dessen raumhohe, doppelt verglaste Fenster den Blick über Wiesen und Felder freigeben, schließt sich im Westen ein Waschraum mit Dusche und WC und im Norden ein überdachter Treppenaufgang aus dem Keller an. Im Süden ist die offene Veranda vorgelagert. Die frei auf Stahlstützen ruhende Deckenkonstruktion hat eine doppelte Schalung mit Kiesklebedach. Die Wände sind außen und innen vertikal mit Holz verschalt; Backsteinfußboden.

1. West side, showing the open veranda which is protected by a glass wall against the prevailing winds.
2. East side, with the ramp leading to the veranda.
3. Sitting room with dining area and veranda.
4, 5. Main floor and basement floor plans. Key: 1 Covered access to basement, 2 Sleeping bunk, 3 Sitting room, 4 Washroom with shower bath and WC, 5 Veranda, 6 Outdoor sitting area, 7 Basement.
6. Sitting room with fireplace; behind the curtain on the left is the sleeping bunk.

1. Westansicht mit der offenen Veranda, die nach der Wetterseite verglast ist.
2. Ostseite mit Rampe zur Veranda.
3. Wohnraum mit Eßplatz und Blick zur Veranda.
4, 5. Grundrisse Wohngeschoß und Kellergeschoß. Legende: 1 Überdachter Zugang zum Keller, 2 Schlafnische, 3 Wohnraum, 4 Waschraum mit Dusche und WC, 5 Veranda, 6 Freisitzplatz, 7 Keller.
6. Wohnraum mit Kamin, links hinter dem Vorhang die Schlafnische.

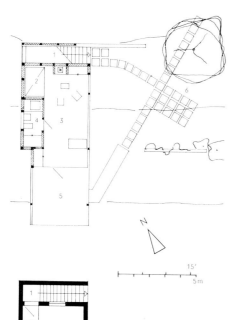

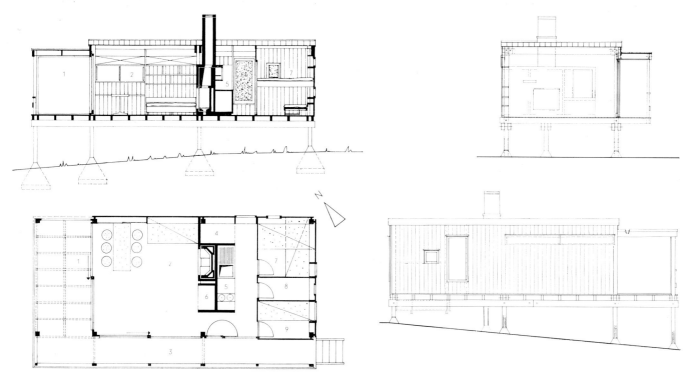

Cottage at Vordemwald near Zofingen, Switzerland

Architects: Atelier 5, Berne
Project designers: E. Fritz, S. Gerber, A. Pini

This small summer cottage, covering an area of no more than 4×8 metres, stands on a slope offering a wide view. It comprises a sitting room with fireplace, a kitchenette, two bedrooms and a WC with shower bath. A loggia along the south-west and north-west sides serves as sun and weather protection for the full-height sliding windows. For economic reasons, the cottage has been constructed in timber. It was also desired to allow for the possibility of dismantling the cottage, and re-erecting it elsewhere, at little cost. The timber frame is supported by concrete piers. The double skin walls and the floor are of spruce boards, insulated with glass fibre. The self-supporting roof consists of two transparent polyester panels placed on a 20 cm high, welded grating with a module of 40× 40 cm.

Ferienhaus in Vordemwald bei Zofingen, Schweiz

Architekten: Atelier 5, Bern
Projektbearbeiter: E. Fritz, S. Gerber, A. Pini

Das kleine Sommerhaus von nur 4×8 m Grundfläche liegt an einem Hang mit weiter Aussicht. Es umfaßt einen Aufenthaltsraum mit Kamin, eine kleine Kochnische, zwei Schlafräume und ein WC mit Dusche. Ein Laufgang längs der Südwest- und Nordwestfassade dient als Sonnen- und Wetterschutz für die raumhohen Schiebefenster. Als Konstruktionsmaterial wurde aus Ersparnisgründen Holz verwendet. Auch sollte die Möglichkeit bestehen, den Bau ohne große Kosten zu demontieren und an anderer Stelle wieder aufzubauen. Das Holzskelett ruht auf Betonsockeln. Die Doppelwände und der Fußboden bestehen aus Tannenholz und sind mit Glasfasern isoliert. Das selbsttragende Dach besteht aus zwei durchsichtigen Polyesterplatten auf einem 20 cm hohen Gitterwerk, dessen geschweißter Raster eine Weite von 40×40 cm hat.

1. Longitudinal section, cross-section, plan and north-east elevation. Key: 1 Covered terrace, 2 Sitting room, 3 Loggia, 4 Cupboard room, 5 Kitchenette, 6 Recess, 7 Master bedroom, 8 WC with shower bath, 9 Children's bedroom.
2. South-west side with loggia and, on the left, the covered terrace. The length of the columns has been adapted to the contours because it was desired to avoid earth movements.
3. West side, with terrace and loggia.
4. Sitting room, with transparent plastic ceiling (top polyester panel blue, bottom panel white). The overhanging roof is lined with spruce fillets throughout.
5. In fine weather, the glass sliding doors can be pushed aside so that sitting room and terrace form a combined outdoor area.
6. Dining area and fireplace corner in the sitting room.

1. Längsschnitt, Querschnitt, Grundriß und Ansicht der Nordostfassade. Legende: 1 Gedeckte Terrasse, 2 Wohnraum, 3 Laufgang und Balkon, 4 Abstellraum, 5 Kochnische, 6 Nische, 7 Eltern, 8 WC mit Dusche, 9 Kinder.
2. Südwestfassade mit Laufgang, links der Balkon. Die Pfosten der Unterkonstruktion sind in ihrer Länge dem Gelände angepaßt, da auf eine Planierung verzichtet wurde.
3. Blick von Westen auf den offenen Balkon und den Laufgang.
4. Wohnraum mit durchscheinender Plastikdecke (obere Polyesterplatte blau, untere weiß). Der auskragende Dachvorsprung ist durchgehend mit Tannenholzriemen verschalt.
5. Bei schönem Wetter lassen sich die Glastüren zurückschieben, so daß Wohnraum und Balkon eine Freifläche bilden.
6. Eßplatz und Kaminecke im Wohnraum.

Cottage of an architect-painter on Cape Cod, Massachusetts

Architect: Serge Chermayeff, New Haven, Connecticut

With this summer cottage which the architect-painter Chermayeff built for himself in a wooded setting on Cape Cod, no attempt has been made to place the house unobtrusively in the landscape. In fact, the building has been deliberately contrasted with its environment by the geometrical treatment of the facade and the bright contrasting colours of the rectangles and triangles. These objects, reminiscent of pennants and parasols, are in keeping with the gay informal atmosphere. There are five 8 ft wide bays, each formed by 'bow-tie truss' frames. The bays are filled with glass or fibre boards criss-crossed by 4 in wide bracing boards. The floor deck, likewise of timber, rests on round concrete pillars. In front of the sitting room is a large planked sun deck on two different levels.

Ferienhaus eines Architekten und Malers auf Cape Cod, Massachusetts

Architekt: Serge Chermayeff, New Haven, Connecticut

Bei dem Ferienhaus, das sich der Architekt und Maler Chermayeff in einem Kiefernwäldchen auf Cape Cod erbaute, ist bewußt darauf verzichtet, das Haus unauffällig in die Landschaft einzupassen. Statt dessen wurde der Baukörper durch die geometrische Fassadenteilung und die leuchtenden Kontrastfarben der Rechtecke und Dreiecksfelder von seiner Umgebung abgesetzt. Die Assoziation von Wimpeln und Sonnenschirmen entspricht der heiteren Ferienatmosphäre. Das Haus besteht aus fünf jeweils 8 Fuß breiten Abteilen, deren Holzrahmenwerk aus Brettbindern sich zum Teil überkreuzt. Die Wandfelder sind mit Glas oder mit Hartfaserplatten ausgefacht, wobei 10 cm breite diagonale Holzlatten für die nötige Aussteifung sorgen. Die ebenfalls in Holzkonstruktion ausgeführte Bodenplatte wird von runden Betonpfeilern getragen. Eine große Plattform aus Holzplanken mit zwei verschiedenen Niveaus ist dem Wohnraum vorgelagert.

1. Entrance side with sun deck. The triangles of the wall panels are in bright red-white, yellow-blue and black-white. The hinged windows are protected by awnings. The timber frame is painted white.
2. Rear side with the sun deck outside the entrance. In the square part of the house on the right are a further bedroom and the studio.
3. The sun deck outside the main frontage.
4. Framing diagram showing the system of 'bow-tie' bracing. (The diagram relates to a different house built to the same principle.)
5. View of living room, with the bedroom in the background. Walls are partly of fibre board, partly faced with diagonally placed boarding.

1. Die Vorderseite mit der vorgesetzten Terrasse. Die Dreiecke der Wandfelder in leuchtendem Rot-Weiß, Gelb-Blau und Schwarz-Weiß. Über den Klappfenstern Sonnenschutzblenden. Holzrahmen weiß bemalt.
2. Die Rückseite mit der Plattform vor dem Eingang. Der quadratische Hausteil rechts enthält einen weiteren Schlafraum und das Atelier.
3. Das Sonnendeck auf der Vorderseite.
4. Schematische Darstellung des Konstruktionssystems aus sich überkreuzenden Brettbindern und diagonal versteiften Wandrahmen. (Das Diagramm bezieht sich auf ein anderes Haus, das nach dem gleichen System erbaut wurde.)
5. Blick in den Wohnraum und den anschließenden Schlafraum. Wände teils aus Hartfaserplatten, teils mit Holzleisten diagonal verschalt.

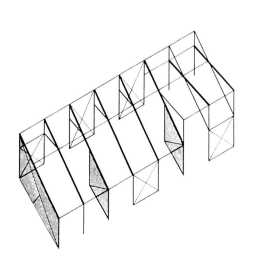

House at Aesch (Hallwiler Lake)

Architect: Max Lüscher-Scolari, Zolliker-berg, Switzerland

This simple, tidily arranged weekend house for a married couple with grown-up children stands on a sparsely wooded site covering 500 sq meters on the eastern shore of Hallwiler Lake. Constructed in timber, the house is placed on concrete piers so that the raised main floor provides a free view across the lake and is protected against rising damp. Below the house is the wine cellar, space for the boat and firewood. All the rooms face west, towards the lake. The measurements conform to Le Corbusier's 'modulor' with 226 cm centres, 456 cm spans, 140 cm cantilever, 226 cm room height (main floor). The tie-and-column structure is held by steel anchors on concrete-filled concrete cylinders. The external walls are of three-ply.

Ferienhaus in Aesch am Hallwiler See

Architekt: Max Lüscher-Scolari, Zolliker-berg, Schweiz

Das einfache, klar gegliederte Ferienhaus für ein Ehepaar mit erwachsenen Kindern wurde auf einem 500 m² großen Grundstück in einem lichten Wäldchen am östlichen Ufer des Hallwiler Sees erbaut. Das aus Holz erstellte Haus ruht auf Betonpfeilern, so daß man vom erhöhten Obergeschoß aus einen freien Blick auf den See hat und keine Bodenfeuchtigkeit eindringen kann. Unter dem Haus befinden sich der Weinkeller und das Boots- und Holzlager. Sämtliche Räume des Obergeschosses sind nach Westen auf den See gerichtet. Die Maße von Grundriß und Konstruktion basieren auf dem Modulor Le Corbusiers: Achsenabstand 226 cm, Spannweite 456 cm, Auskragung 140 cm, Raumhöhe im Obergeschoß 226 cm. Die Zangen- und Ständerkonstruktion ist durch eiserne Fußanker auf die ausbetonierten Zementröhren abgestützt. Die Außenwände sind dreischalig ausgebildet.

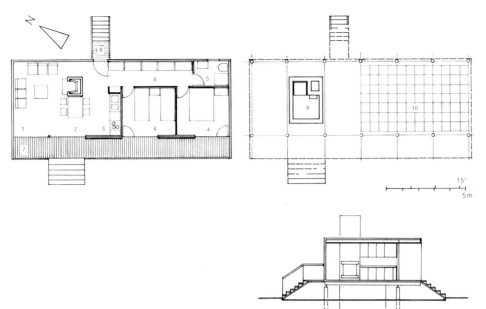

1, 3, 4. See following page.
2. Main floor plan (left), lower floor plan (right), and cross-section (bottom). Key: 1 Sitting room, 2 Dining area, 3 Kitchenette, 4 Bedrooms, 5 WC, 6 Cupboards, 7 Loggia, 8 Entrance, 9 Wine cellar, 10 Space for boat and firewood.

1, 3, 4 siehe folgende Seite.
2. Grundriß von Wohngeschoß (links), Untergeschoß (rechts) und Querschnitt (unten). Legende: 1 Wohnraum, 2 Eßplatz, 3 Kochnische, 4 Schlafräume, 5 Toilette, 6 Schränke, 7 Loggia, 8 Eingang, 9 Weinkeller, 10 Boots- und Holzlager.

1. (Page 32) West side, seen from the lake. Square, room-height sliding shutters, protecting the four windows, are shown open; they are suspended and two adjacent panels can be pushed in front of a windowless panel. They consist of wood fibreboard sandwiched between white glazed asbestos cement panels.

3. (Page 33) West side, seen from the lakeside meadow.

4. (Page 33) West side, closed by the sliding shutters which serve as a burglar protection when the owners are absent.

5. Apart from the entrance door, the north and east sides are entirely covered by vertical timber boarding.

6. View from the sitting room across the lake. The loggia on the west side provides sun and weather protection.

7. Dining area beside the fireplace, with the kitchenette in the background.

1. (Seite 32) Die Westfassade vom See aus. Die raumhohen quadratischen Schiebewände vor den vier Fenstern sind geöffnet, wobei immer zwei Wände hintereinander vor einen fest verschalten Teil geschoben werden. Die Schiebewände bestehen aus Holzfaserplatten mit aufgedoppelten weißen Glanzeternitplatten. Sie sind oben aufgehängt und haben eine Einfassung aus Kulisseeisen.

3. (Seite 33) Westseite mit Liegewiese.

4. (Seite 33) Westfassade mit geschlossenen Schiebewänden, die das Haus in unbewohnten Zeiten gegen Einbruch schützen.

5. Die bis auf die Eingangstür völlig geschlossene Nord- und Ostfassade mit senkrechter Holzschalung.

6. Ausblick vom Wohnraum auf den See. Die der Westfassade vorgebaute Loggia dient als Sonnen- und Wetterschutz.

7. Eßplatz am freistehenden Kamin.

House with Sauna at Puumala, Eastern Finland

Architects: Marjatta and Martti Jaatinen, Tapiola

This house, constructed exclusively of wood, stands in the midst of the woods by one of the countless Finnish lakes. Because it is only used during the summer, no thermal insulation has been provided; walls, ceiling and floors consist of simple raw spruce boards. When the house is not in use, the verandas are enclosed by wooden sliding shutters running on metal rails. The roof structure consists of nailed rafters. A separate building, also wood, contains a garage for two cars, a basement and store room. The sauna, placed some distance from the house, is also used during the winter and has therefore been constructed of solid timber beams. It stands slightly above the lake which can be reached by a wooden flight of stairs and a gangway. The sympathetic integration with its environment is the special attraction of this house.

Ferienhaus mit Sauna in Puumala, Ostfinnland

Architekten: Marjatta und Martti Jaatinen, Tapiola

Das als reiner Holzbau konstruierte Ferienhaus liegt mitten im Wald an einem der vielen Seen der finnischen Seenplatte. Da es nur im Sommer benutzt wird, konnte auf jede Wärmeisolierung verzichtet werden; Wände, Decke und Fußboden bestehen aus einfachen rohen Tannenbrettern. Ist das Haus unbewohnt, so werden in Metallschienen laufende Holzwände vor die Veranden geschoben. Genagelte Holzbinder bilden die Dachkonstruktion. Die ebenfalls aus Holzbrettern gebaute Doppelgarage mit Keller und Vorratsraum steht für sich in der Nähe des Hauses. Die etwas abseits gelegene Sauna wird auch im Winter benutzt und ist deshalb aus festen Holzbalken errichtet. Sie steht etwas höher als der See, den man über eine Holztreppe und einen Steg erreicht. Die harmonische Eingliederung in die Landschaft macht den besonderen Reiz des Hauses aus.

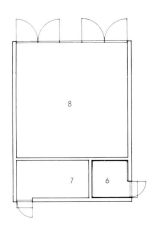
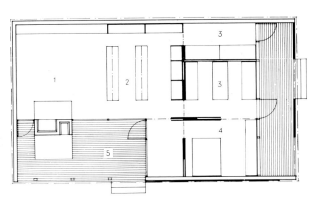

Key: 1 Living room, 2 Kitchen, 3 Bedroom, 4 Master bedroom, 5 Veranda, 6 Basement, 7 Store room, 8 Garage for two cars, 9 Entrance hall, 10 Sauna, 11 Changing and heating room.

Legende: 1 Wohnraum, 2 Küche, 3 Schlafraum, 4 Elternschlafraum, 5 Veranda, 6 Keller, 7 Vorratsraum, 8 Doppelgarage, 9 Vorraum, 10 Sauna, 11 Umkleide- und Heizraum.

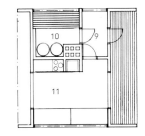

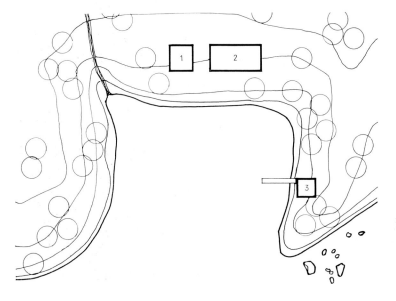

1. (Page 35) View across the lake on the south side of the house, with the veranda.
2. Plan of garage (top left), house (top right) and sauna (bottom).
3, 4. East side of the house, with closed and open sliding shutters respectively.
5. Site plan: 1 Garage, 2 House, 3 Sauna.
6. West side, with the clerestory windows of the sitting room.
7. Sauna with gangway.

1. (Seite 35) Blick über den See auf die Südseite mit der offenen Veranda.
2. Grundriß Garage (oben links), Wohnhaus (oben rechts) und Sauna.
3, 4. Ostseite mit geschlossenen und geöffneten Schiebeläden.
5. Lageplan: 1 Garage, 2 Haus, 3 Sauna.
6. Westseite mit dem Oberlichtband des Wohnraumes.
7. Sauna mit Laufsteg.

8. Main veranda. In the centre is the two-faced fireplace, facing the veranda as well as the lounge. Above the otherwise windowless wall of the west side is a narrow strip of clerestory window. When the house is not in use, the veranda is enclosed by large wooden shutters running on rails.
9. The sitting room is separated from the south veranda by an L-shaped glass partition. The indoor side of the two-faced fireplace can be seen in the centre.
10. Dining area in the north-western corner of the house.
11. The kitchen is freely placed in the sitting room. The top cupboard unit is suspended on angle irons from the roof joists. On the left is the cupboard wall of the sitting room area and the kitchen.

8. Blick auf die Hauptveranda des Hauses. In der Mitte der Kombinationskamin mit zwei Feueröffnungen zur Veranda und zum Innenraum hin. Über der geschlossenen Holzwand der Westseite ein schmales Oberlichtband. Ist das Haus nicht bewohnt, so werden große, auf Schienen laufende Holztafeln vor die offene Seite der Veranda geschoben.
9. Der Wohnraum ist von der Südveranda durch eine L-förmige Glaswand getrennt. In der Bildmitte ist die dem Wohnraum zugewandte Feueröffnung des Doppelkamins zu erkennen.
10. Der Eßplatz in der Nordwestecke,
11. Die Küche ist frei in den Wohnraum gestellt. Der Oberschrank wurde an Winkeleisen vom Dachbinder abgehängt. Links die Schrankwand von Wohnraum und Küchenbereich.

Summer house at Rust (Neusiedler Lake)

Architect: Bruno Tinhofer, Vienna

This house has been erected on a pre-existing platform supported on piles. The plan consists of two main sections: the daytime rooms facing east, with kitchen, shower bath and cupboard room, and the bedroom wing facing west, with two bedrooms, each for three people. Between the two sections is a covered but otherwise open space, extended by an open terrace facing the lake. This opening and the glass door frontage of the sitting room can be closed by sliding shutters. As a protection against burglars, mesh steel reinforcement is inserted in walls, ceiling and floor. The WC is outside, hidden in the high reeds, reached by a plankway. A boat house is attached on the north side, facing the shore. Construction: timber framework; walls faced with white asbestos cement; reed panels serving as thermal insulation; flat roof of aluminium sheeting.

Sommerhaus bei Rust am Neusiedler See

Architekt: Bruno Tinhofer, Wien

Das Haus wurde auf einer schon vorhandenen Grundplatte auf Pfählen errichtet. Der Grundriß gliedert sich in zwei Hauptteile: den nach Osten liegenden Wohnteil mit Küche, Dusche und Abstellraum und den nach Westen orientierten Schlafteil mit zwei Schlafräumen für je drei Personen. Beide Teile sind durch einen gedeckten Freiraum miteinander verbunden, dem zum See hin eine offene Terrasse vorgelagert ist. Diese Öffnung und die Glastürfront des Wohnzimmers können durch Schiebetore geschlossen werden. Baustahlgitter in Wänden, Fußböden und Decken sichern gegen Einbruch. Das Klosett liegt abseits im Schilf und ist durch einen Steg erreichbar. Auf der Landseite ist ein Bootshaus angebaut. Konstruktion: Holzskelett, Wandflächen mit weißen Eternitplatten verkleidet, Schilfplatten zur Wärmeisolation, Flachdach mit Aluminium gedeckt.

1. South-west side, with open terrace and living room. On the left are the bedrooms and, behind them, the boat house. To the south of the bedroom wing is the sliding shutter by which the covered terrace can be closed. The open terrace is protected by removable blinds.
2. South-east side. The east side clerestory windows mark living room and kitchen.
3. Plan. Key: 1 Access, and plankway leading to the WC, 2 Boat house, 3 Covered terrace, 4 Living-cum-dining room, 5 Kitchen, 6 Shower-bath, 7 Cupboard room, 8 Open terrace, 9 Bedroom, 10 Boat pier.
4. Lakeside terrace. On the left, the sitting room windows. The outside of the reed balustrade has asbestos cement facing.
5. Sitting room with clerestory windows. Walls faced with untreated boards.
6. The sitting room windows are here covered by the asbestos cement shutters.

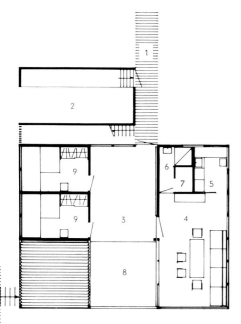

1. Seeseite von Südwesten mit offener Terrasse und Wohnraum. Links die Schlafzimmer, dahinter das angebaute Bootshaus. Vor der Südseite des Schlafteils das Schiebetor, das die gedeckte Terrasse freigibt. Über der offenen Terrasse mobile Sonnenschutzlamellen.
2. Südostansicht. An der Schmalseite das Oberlichtband von Wohnraum und Küche.
3. Grundriß. Legende: 1 Zugang und Steg zum Klosett, 2 Bootshaus, 3 gedeckter Freiraum, 4 Wohn- und Eßraum, 5 Küche, 6 Dusche, 7 Abstellraum, 8 offene Terrasse, 9 Schlafraum, 10 Bootssteg.
4. Die offene Terrasse zum See. Links die Glaswand des Wohnraums, Schilfbrüstung außen mit Eternitplatten verkleidet.
5. Wohnraum mit Oberlichtband. Wände mit Naturholzdielen verschalt.
6. Vor die Glasfront des Wohnraums ist das Tor aus Eternitplatten geschoben.

**Summer houses on the Helgenæs
Peninsula, Denmark**

Architects: Knud Friis and Elmar Moltke
Nielsen, Aarhus

These two Danish houses are distinguished by their deliberately simple and unpretentious design and appointments. The coarse textured outer walls to east, north and south, cast in sea sand, shells and cement, the minute windows, the natural timber doors with stable door fittings, the round timber roofing, the white-washed inner walls and the rustic, tiled floors are deliberately chosen to suggest stables or barns. Everything is designed to create an informal atmosphere and to simplify the housework as much as possible. Facing west, the room-height windows of the sitting room afford a wide view over the landscape. Wind protection and privacy for the sun terrace outside the sitting room is ensured by a free-standing concrete wall. An open porch is provided at the south-east corner.

**Sommerhäuser auf der Halbinsel
Helgenæs, Dänemark**

Architekten: Knud Friis und Elmar Moltke
Nielsen, Aarhus

Die beiden dänischen Ferienhäuser sind durch die bewußte Einfachheit und Anspruchslosigkeit ihrer Anlage und Inneneinrichtung gekennzeichnet. Die groben Außenmauern der Ost-, Süd- und Nordseite aus Seesand, Muscheln und Zement mit den winzigen Fensteröffnungen, die rohen Brettertüren mit ihren Stalltürbeschlägen, die Rundholzüberdachung, die weißgekalkten Innenwände und die derben Ziegelfußböden sollen an Ställe oder Scheunen erinnern. Alles ist darauf abgestimmt, eine ungezwungene, informelle Ferienatmosphäre zu schaffen und die Hausarbeit so weit wie möglich zu vereinfachen. Nach Westen gewähren die raumhohen Fenster des Wohnraums einen freien Ausblick in die Landschaft. Die vorgelagerte Sonnenterrasse wird durch eine freistehende Betonmauer vor Nordwind und Einblick geschützt. An der Südostecke ist eine offene Vorhalle angebaut, die als Spiel- und Trockenplatz dient.

1. West side; fully glazed living room and, behind strip windows (right), bedrooms.
2. The houses seen from the north.
3. Enclosed east side with small kitchen and living room windows.
4. Plan: 1 Porch, 2 Entrance, 3 Bathroom and WC, 4 Kitchen, 5 Master bedroom, 6 Bedroom, 7 Dining area, 8 Fireplace, 9 Sitting room, 10 Outdoor sitting area.

1. Westfront mit dem voll verglasten Wohnraum, rechts hinter Fensterband Schlafräume.
2. Die beiden Häuser von Norden.
3. Die geschlossene Ostseite mit den kleinen Fensteröffnungen von Küche und Wohnraum.
4. Grundriß: 1 Überdeckte Vorhalle, 2 Eingang, 3 Bad und WC, 4 Küche, 5 Elternschlafraum, 6 Schlafraum, 7 Eßplatz, 8 Kamin, 9 Wohnraum, 10 Freisitzplatz.

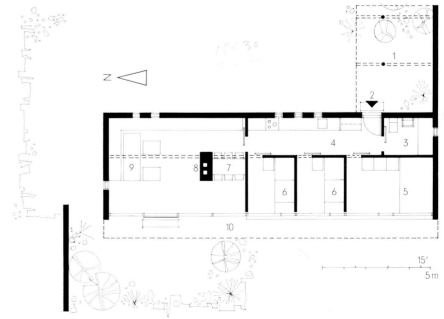

5. From the entrance (on the left behind the cupboard) one enters a long corridor-cum-kitchen. The coarse brick floor is easily cleaned.
6. Sitting corner in the living room. The bench extends along the whole width of the room. The dark-stained round timbers of the ceiling provide a contrast with the bright tones of the untreated wall boards.
7. View towards the east. The concrete screen wall ensures privacy.

5. Vom Eingang aus (hinter dem Schrank links) betritt man einen langen Verbindungsflur, in den zugleich die Küche eingebaut ist. Der grobe Backsteinfußboden ist leicht sauberzuhalten.
6. Sitzecke im Wohnraum. Die Bank nimmt die ganze Breite des Raumes ein. Die dunklen Rundbalken der Decke kontrastieren mit der hellen Naturholzverschalung der Wände.
7. Blick nach Osten. Die Sichtschutzmauer trennt die benachbarten Grundstücke.

8. One of the sleeping cabins. The upper bed is suspended from the roof joist, the lower bed rests on a brick foundation.
9. The dining area is inserted between wall and fireplace. Partitions and ceilings are plastered. The sliding doors have stable door fittings.

8. Eine der Schlafkojen. Das obere Bett ist an einem Deckenbalken aufgehängt. Der untere Bettrahmen ruht auf einem Backsteinsockel.
9. Der Eßplatz ist zwischen Wand und Kaminblock eingespannt. Die Zwischenwände und die Decke sind mit Kalk beworfen. Schiebetüren mit Stalltürbeschlägen.

House at Bridgehampton, Long Island

Architect: Peter Blake, New York

This house, built by the architect for his own use, stands on a headland on the south coast of Long Island. It is a simple, tidily arranged framed structure of steel, wood and glass which, being close to the Atlantic and, during hurricanes, almost within reach of the waves, has been placed on a platform. To reduce the resistance offered to the hurricanes and to enable the house to be integrated with the landscape as much as possible, the space in the centre between the square blocks, containing the living rooms and bedrooms respectively, has been left open. But if it should also be desired to use the house during the winter, this space can be closed in by glass walls. The accommodation includes a sitting room and four bedrooms for the parents and three children, as well as bathroom and WC. The house is surrounded by a covered walkway. On the east and west sides, the open passage ends in open sun decks.

Ferienhaus bei Bridgehampton auf Long Island

Architekt: Peter Blake, New York

Auf einer Landzunge an der Südküste von Long Island hat sich der Architekt sein eigenes Ferienhaus erbaut: eine einfache, klare Rahmenkonstruktion aus Stahl, Holz und Glas, die wegen der Nähe des Atlantiks, dessen Wellen bei Sturm fast bis an das Haus heranreichen, auf eine Plattform gestellt wurde. Um den Hurrikans weniger Widerstand zu bieten und um die Landschaft so weit wie möglich in das Haus hereinzuholen, blieb der Mittelgang zwischen den quadratischen Blöcken mit den Wohn- und Schlafräumen offen; er kann jedoch, falls das Haus auch im Winter bewohnt werden sollte, durch Glaswände zu einer Art Patio geschlossen werden. Das Raumprogramm umfaßt einen gemeinsamen Aufenthaltsraum und vier Schlafzimmer für die Eltern und drei Kinder sowie Bad und WC. Eine gedeckte Plattform läuft rings um das Haus. Im Osten und Westen mündet der offene Durchgang auf ungedeckte Sonnenterrassen.

44

1–3. East side (Fig 1), west side (Fig 2), and west-side terrace (Fig 3). The steel frame of the house consists of twelve cylindrical columns carrying six ⊥-beams which support the roof. Wooden wall panels alternate with full-height, glass sliding doors and fixed windows so that sections of the sweeping coastal landscape become part of the house as if they were framed pictures. It is planned to protect the glass panels by additional wood shutters.

4. Plan. Key: 1 Sitting room, 2 Kitchen unit, 3 Open passage, 4 Master bedroom, 5 Children's bedroom, 6 Bathroom and WC, 7 Covered walkway, 8 Sun deck.

1–3. Ostseite (Abb. 1), Westseite (Abb. 2) und Westterrasse (Abb. 3). Das Stahlgerüst des Hauses besteht aus 12 Rohrstützen mit 6 ⊥-Trägern, auf denen das Dach ruht. Holzwandfelder wechseln mit raumhohen Glasschiebetüren und feststehenden Glaswänden, durch die Ausschnitte der weiten Küstenlandschaft wie gerahmte Bilder in das Haus einbezogen werden. Es ist vorgesehen, das Haus durch zusätzliche Holzschutzwände vor den Glasflächen zu sichern.

4. Grundriß. Legende: 1 Wohnraum, 2 Küchenblock, 3 offener Durchgang, 4 Elternschlafzimmer, 5 Kinderzimmer, 6 Bad und WC, 7 gedeckte Plattform, 8 offene Sonnenterrasse.

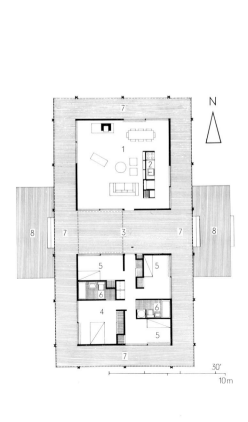

5. Sea view across the sun deck.
6. Like all other rooms, the master bedroom has a direct sliding door connection with the walkway surrounding the house.
7. As most activities are outdoors, the children's bedrooms have been kept small.
8. Kitchen unit, flanked by the dining area.
9. Floor, ceiling and walls of the sitting room are covered with narrow boarding.

5. Blick über das westliche Sonnendeck.
6. Wie sämtliche Räume ist auch das Elternschlafzimmer durch eine Schiebetür direkt mit der Außengalerie verbunden.
7. Da sich das Leben meist im Freien abspielt, genügen kleine Kinderzimmer.
8. Küchenblock, daneben der Eßplatz.
9. Fußboden, Decke und Wände des Wohnraums sind mit schmalen Holzriemen verschalt.

House at Galapos near Lisbon

Architect: Eduardo Anahory, Paris

On the rocky Atlantic coast twenty-five miles from Lisbon, the architect has built his own house, making use as far as possible of prefabricated components. Construction and materials had to be strong enough to resist waves and storms. The house has therefore been anchored to the rock by means of steel supports on concrete foundations. A steel platform covering approximately 23 × 55 ft carries a pinewood frame structure with wall panels of pressed cork. On the outside, these panels are protected by a coating of white plastic varnish. Cork has also been used for the indoor partitions and for the roof panels which are covered with bituminous felt but are left untreated on the inside. The bedrooms as well as kitchen and two bathrooms are combined in a compact core.

Ferienhaus in Galapos bei Lissabon

Architekt: Eduardo Anahory, Paris

An der Steilküste des Atlantik, 40 km von Lissabon, baute sich der Architekt ein Ferienhaus, bei dem weitgehend vorfabrizierte Teile verwendet sind. Konstruktion und Material mußten gewährleisten, daß es der Brandung und den Stürmen widerstehen konnte. Deshalb wurde es auf Stahlstützen mit Betonfundamenten im Felsgrund verankert. Auf einer aus Metallprofilen konstruierten Plattform von rund 7 × 17 m ist eine Rahmenkonstruktion aus Pinienholz errichtet, die mit Wandfeldern aus gepreßter Korkeiche ausgefacht wurde. Die Außenseite der Wandtafeln erhielt einen Schutzanstrich aus weißem Kunststofflack. Aus Kork sind auch die Trennwände im Inneren und die 10 cm dicken Dachplatten, die außen mit Bitumenpappe abgedeckt und innen roh belassen wurden. Die Schlafräume für Eltern und Kinder sowie die Küche und zwei Badezimmer sind in einem kompakten Block zusammengefaßt.

48

1. View from the sea. On the left the large terrace outside the sitting room; on the right the compact core with bedrooms, bathrooms and kitchen.
2. View from the beach, with view of the platform from below.
3. Section and plan. Key: 1 Entrance, 2 Sitting room with fireplace, 3 Terrace, 4 Kitchen, 5 Children's bedroom, 6 Master bedroom.
4. At low tide, the house stands on its steel columns high above the beach.

1. Frontalansicht. Links die große Aussichtsterrasse vor dem Wohnraum, rechts der geschlossene Block mit Schlafräumen, Bädern und Küche.
2. Blick vom Strand unter die Plattform.
3. Schnitt und Grundriß. Legende: 1 Eingang, 2 Wohnraum mit Kamin, 3 Terrasse, 4 Küche, 5 Kinder, 6 Eltern.
4. Bei Ebbe steht das Haus auf seinen Stahlstützen hoch über dem Strand.

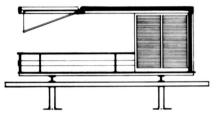

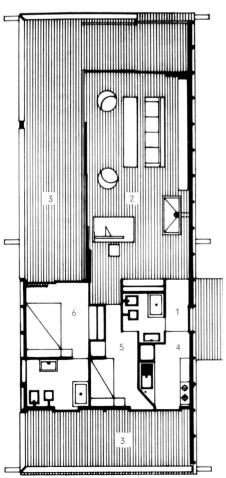

49

5. By pushing back the sliding doors visible in the centre of the picture, the sitting room can be enlarged to twice its width. This can be done by tilting up the shutters which serve both as a sun protection and as a protection against burglars. Between the roof joists, a gap has been kept open to permit air circulation. The glass door on the right leads to the master bedroom.

6. Sitting room, with the sliding doors open. The open fireplace in the foreground can be dismantled during the summer.

5. Durch Zurückschieben der in der Bildmitte sichtbaren Schiebetüren kann der Wohnraum auf das Doppelte verbreitert werden. Dies geschieht durch Hochklappen der Lamellenläden, die sowohl als Sonnenschutz wie als Sicherung gegen Einbrecher dienen. Zwischen den Tragbalken der Dachkonstruktion ist ein Spalt zur Luftzirkulation offen gelassen. Die Glastür rechts führt in das Elternschlafzimmer.

6. Blick in den Wohnraum bei geöffneter Schiebewand. Der im Vordergrund sichtbare offene Kamin kann im Sommer demontiert werden.

1. Sitting room. The full-height windows on the east and south sides afford a wide view across the Øresund.

1. Blick in den Wohnraum. Durch die raumhohen Glaswände hat man eine weite Aussicht über den Øresund.

House at the Øresund

Architect: Anders Grum, Birkerød, Denmark

In designing his house on the Øresund, the architect was anxious to achieve sympathy between house and landscape. He placed an oblong building on the edge of a cliff some 230 ft from the sea. The north side, close to the northern boundary of the plot, is without windows. Because of the rough and variable climate, protected outdoor spaces are recessed into the house. A covered terrace has thus been provided outside the three bedrooms on the south side; similarly, the east terrace outside the sitting room has also been covered. On the north and west sides, the roof is supported by white plastered brick walls, and on the south and east sides by timber posts. The south bedroom front is faced with wooden boards. Indoor partitions, ceiling and floor are of deal.

Ferienhaus am Øresund

Architekt: Anders Grum, Birkerød, Dänemark

Beim Entwurf seines eigenen Ferienhauses am Øresund kam es dem Architekten vor allem auf den Zusammenklang zwischen Architektur und Natur an. Er stellte den langgestreckten Bau etwa 70 m landeinwärts an die Kante eines Hanges, der steil zum Strand abfällt. Die Nordseite ist als geschlossene Front der nördlichen Grundstücksgrenze zugewandt. Wegen des rauhen und wechselhaften Küstenklimas wurden geschützte Freiräume in den Hauskörper einbezogen. So ist den drei Schlafräumen nach Süden eine überdeckte Terrasse vorgelagert, und auch die Ostterrasse vor dem Wohnraum wurde überdacht. Im Norden und Westen wird das Dach von weiß verputzten Ziegelmauern getragen, auf der Süd- und Ostseite ruht es auf Holzpfosten. Die Südfront ist vor den Schlafräumen mit Holzbrettern verschalt. Im Inneren bestehen Wände, Decke und Fußboden aus roh belassenen Tannenholzdielen.

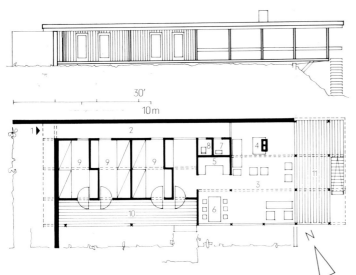

2. The east side of the house seen from the beach.
3. South-eastern corner, with a view across the Øresund towards the Swedish coast. In the foreground, behind the brick wall, an open veranda outside the bedrooms, followed by three window bays of the sitting room. The last bay is taken up by an open balcony on the east side.
4. South elevation and plan. Key: 1 Entrance, 2 Corridor, 3 Sitting room, 4 Fireplace, 5 Kitchen, 6 Dining area, 7 Bathroom, 8 WC, 9 Bedroom, 10 South terrace, 11 Balcony.
5. South side.

2. Vom Strand aus gesehen liegt die Ostseite des Hauses hinter Bäumen geschützt.
3. Die Südostecke mit Blick über den Sund auf das schwedische Festland. Im Vordergrund hinter der Ziegelmauer die offene Veranda vor den Schlafräumen, anschließend die drei Fensterfelder des Wohnraums. In der letzten Stützenachse der offene Ostbalkon.
4. Südansicht und Grundriß: 1 Eingang, 2 Flur, 3 Wohnraum, 4 Kamin, 5 Küche, 6 Eßplatz, 7 Bad, 8 WC, 9 Schlafraum, 10 Terrasse, 11 Balkon.
5. Gesamtansicht von Süden.

6. Dining area and kitchenette, seen from the living room. The dark-stained posts and joists are in contrast with the light deal boards covering ceiling and floor.

6. Blick vom Wohnraum auf Eßplatz und Kochnische. Die dunkel behandelte Holzkonstruktion der Stützen und Deckenbalken kontrastiert mit dem hellen Tannenholz von Wänden, Decke und Fußboden.

7. Two sleeping cabins; the one in the rear has additional top lighting. On the right, built-in cupboards.
8. Covered south terrace with the entrances to the bedrooms. Between the two doors are the wooden shutters which can be folded back.

7. Zwei Schlafkojen, von denen die hintere durch ein Oberlicht zusätzlich beleuchtet wird. Rechts eingebaute Wandschränke.
8. Die gedeckte Südterrasse mit den Zugängen zum Schlafteil. Zwischen den beiden Türen die seitlich schwenkbaren Holzläden.

1–4. Overall view. The south side of the guest house at different times of the year, and in different stages of use. When not in use, the house is protected by the closed shutters and wooden doors. If the house is used for a short time only, the shutters may remain closed so that entry of daylight is confined to the glass doors behind the wooden doors which are swung outwards. Normally, the 2×2 m shutters are swung upwards by 90° and fastened to a beam mounted on cantilevered joists 1 metre in front of the facade (Fig 6). In this position, the shutters also serve as sun and weather protection. When open, the 1 metre wide wooden doors serve as screens between two adjacent pairs of rooms. In fine weather, the glass doors can be swung inwards and folded up so that the rooms are completely open towards the park.

1–4. Gesamtansicht. Die Südseite des Gästehauses in verschiedenen Jahreszeiten und Stadien. Das unbewohnte Haus ist durch die geschlossenen Klappläden und Holztüren geschützt. Bei vorübergehender Benutzung können die Klappläden geschlossen bleiben und die Räume durch die Glastüren hinter den nach vorn geschwenkten Holztüren belichtet werden. Normalerweise werden die 2×2 m großen Klappläden um 90° nach oben geschwenkt und an einem Überzug, der an Kragbalken 1 m vor die Fassade gesetzt ist, befestigt (Abb. 6). Die hochgeklappten Läden dienen zugleich als Sonnen- und Wetterschutz. Die 1 m breiten Holztüren bilden in geöffnetem Zustand Schirmwände zwischen jeweils zwei Zimmerpaaren. Bei schönem Wetter können die Glastüren nach innen gefaltet werden, so daß die Räume völlig offen sind.

Guest house at Tibirke, Denmark

Architect: Vilhelm Wohlert, Copenhagen

The guest house, erected for the Danish nuclear physicist Niels Bohr in the park of his own summer house on the north coast of Zeeland, comprises two single bedrooms, two double bedrooms for children, a room for the children's nurse, a lavatory and a shower bath. Kitchen facilities have not been provided as the meals are taken in the main building. The guest house has a timber structure raised above the ground by three concrete strip foundations. The outer walls are faced with varnished deal boards, the inner walls have a coating of white oil paint; there is timber flooring. The module governing the width and depth of the rooms is based on the size of the beds and each room is three times as wide and twice as long as a bed. All four guest rooms face south and can be opened up by raising the large (4 sq metres) shutters and pushing back the glass folding doors.

Gästehaus in Tibirke, Dänemark

Architekt: Vilhelm Wohlert, Kopenhagen

Das Gästehaus, das der dänische Atomphysiker Niels Bohr im Park seines eigenen Sommerhauses südlich des Kattegatt errichten ließ, umfaßt zwei Einbettzimmer, zwei Zweibettzimmer für Kinder und einen Raum für das Kindermädchen nebst einer Toilette und einem Duschraum. Auf eine Kochnische wurde verzichtet, da die Mahlzeiten im Haupthaus eingenommen werden. Der Bau ist eine Holzkonstruktion, die auf drei Streifenfundamenten aus Beton vom Terrain abgehoben ist. Sie ist außen mit lasierten Tannenbrettern verschalt, die Innenwände sind mit weißer Ölfarbe gestrichen; Bretterfußboden. Als Modul für Breite und Tiefe der Räume dienten die Bettenmaße. Jedes Zimmer ist dreimal so breit und doppelt so lang wie ein Bett. Sämtliche vier Gastzimmer, die alle nach Süden orientiert sind, lassen sich auf der Frontseite vollständig öffnen.

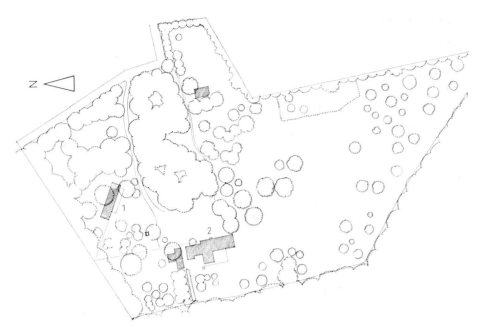

5. Site plan. The guest house (1) stands some distance away from the main building (2), at an angle of 60°, in order to enable the guests to be on their own, yet to preserve the visual connection with the older summer house – a converted farmhouse, which has set the scale for the new building.

5. Lageplan. Das Gästehaus (1) wurde in einem Winkel von 60° in einiger Entfernung vom Hauptgebäude (2) errichtet, um den Gästen die Möglichkeit zu geben, für sich zu sein und trotzdem die optische Verbindung mit dem alten, aus einem Bauernhaus umgebauten Ferienhaus aufrechtzuerhalten, das als maßstabgebende Baukulisse für den Neubau diente.

6. The wooden entrance doors are open and the shutters drawn up. Above the fascia board is a strip of clerestory lighting with ventilation louvres over the width of the doors.

6. Hier sind die hölzernen Eingangstüren zur Seite gedreht und die Läden hochgeklappt. Über dem Stirnbrett verläuft ein Oberlichtband, das in Türbreite mit einem Ventilationsgitter ausgerüstet wurde.

56

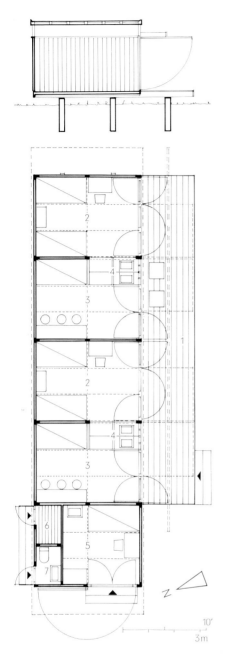

7. Cross-section and plan. Key: 1 Terrace, 2 Bedroom with two beds, 3 Bedroom with one bed, 4 Built-in cupboard and wash basin, 5 Nurse's room, 6 Shower bath, 7 WC.

8. South side with open shutters and doors.

9. South-east corner. The room is entered through the single-leaf glass door. The windows shows the mirror reflection of the thatched main building.

10. During the winter, the entrance to the nurse's room at the western end of the house is protected by a wooden folding door.

7. Querschnitt und Grundriß. Legende: 1 Terrasse, 2 Zweibettzimmer, 3 Einbettzimmer, 4 Einbauschrank und Waschbekken, 5 Mädchenzimmer, 6 Dusche, 7 WC.

8. Südfront bei geöffneten Läden und Türen. Hinter den feststehenden Wandteilen aus undurchsichtigem Glas liegen die Waschbecken.

9. Wandausschnitt der Südfassade. Man betritt das Zimmer durch die einflügelige Glastür. Im Fenster das Spiegelbild des strohgedeckten Haupthauses.

10. Der Eingang zum Mädchenzimmer auf der Giebelseite wird im Winter durch eine Holzklapptür geschützt.

House in Westchester County, New York

Architect: I. M. Pei, New York, N. Y.

This house, which the architect built for his own family (two adults and four children) in the undulating countryside of Westchester County north of New York, provides more freedom of movement than might be expected in a plan area of no more than 1,000 sq ft or so. The structure consisting of glued timber beams and posts, is raised above the sloping site on eight pillars which were erected in one day. The roof was mounted in a week without the aid of specialist craftsmen. Everything has been so designed that, in spite of the four children and many guests, the housewife can manage without help. The interior consists of a heatable core with bedrooms, a large sitting room where winter weekends are spent and a surrounding partly glazed porch which is connected by sliding glass panels with the sitting and bedrooms.

Wochenend- und Ferienhaus in Westchester County, New York

Architekt: I. M. Pei, New York, N. Y.

Das Wochenend- und Ferienhaus, das sich der Architekt für seine Familie (zwei Erwachsene und vier Kinder) nördlich von New York in dem Hügelland der Westchester County erbaute, gibt den Bewohnern weit mehr Bewegungsfreiheit, als die bebaute Fläche von nur etwa 92 m² vermuten ließe. Auf dem unplanierten Baugrund wurde der Rahmen aus verleimten Holzbindern und -pfosten auf acht Stützen vom Terrain abgehoben und an einem einzigen Tag montiert. Auch das Dach wurde ohne Facharbeiter in sieben Tagen fertiggestellt. Alles ist so geplant, daß die Hausfrau trotz der vier Kinder und vieler Gäste ohne Hilfe auskommt. Das Innere besteht aus einem heizbaren Kern mit den Schlafzimmern und einem großen Wohnraum, in denen man im Winter das Wochenende verbringt, und der umlaufenden, teilweise verglasten, durch Glasschiebetüren erreichbare Terrasse.

1. View from the west-side terrace towards the wooded hills. The deal floor boards are hosed down for cleaning.
2. Front view, with the wooden approach bridge.
3. Close-up of entrance side with north-west corner.

1. Blick von der Terrasse auf der Westseite auf das bewaldete Hügelland. Die Tannenholzdielen werden zur Reinigung mit dem Schlauch abgespritzt.
2. Frontalansicht mit dem Zugang über eine Holzbrücke.
3. Detailansicht der Eingangsseite mit der Nordwestecke.

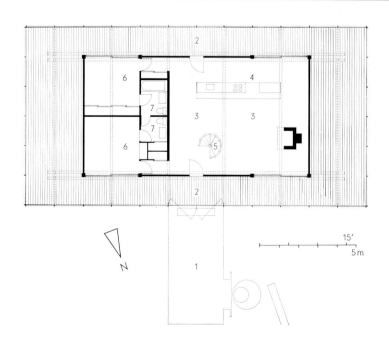

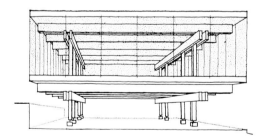

4. Perspective of the timber structure.
5. Plan. Key: 1 Wooden bridge, 2 Porch, 3 Living room, 4 Kitchen, 5 Spiral stairs, 6 Bedroom, 7 Bathroom and WC.

4. Perspektive der Holzkonstruktion.
5. Grundriß. Legende: 1 Holzbrücke, 2 Terrasse, 3 Wohnraum, 4 Küche, 5 Wendeltreppe, 6 Schlafraum, 7 Bad und WC.

15'
5 m

N

6. Daylight enters the large living room through the sliding glass panels and a skylight with special sun protection. The open, island-type fireplace is erected of brick, and white-washed. Through the well-like shaft, seen on the right, spiral stairs lead down to the gravel-surfaced open space below the house.

7. The back of the shoulder-high cabinet unit in the living room is designed as a kitchen unit. The floor is covered with dark teak boards.

6. Der große Wohnraum empfängt sein Tageslicht durch die Glasschiebetüren und ein mit einem Sonnenschutz versehenes Oberlicht. Der gemauerte, weiß getünchte Kamin steht frei im Raum. Durch den brunnenähnlichen Schacht rechts führt eine Wendeltreppe hinab zu dem kiesbestreuten offenen Raum unter dem Haus.

7. Der schulterhohe Schrank im Wohnraum ist auf der Rückseite als Küchenblock ausgebildet. Der Fußboden besteht aus dunklen Teakholzdielen.

8. One of the two bedrooms. The glass sliding doors have aluminium frames and wooden blinds. Behind the chequered cupboard wall with panels of Japanese paper is the second bedroom. Every night, the children roll their beds into a position which they choose themselves.
9. East side of porch with dining area. All details have been designed with meticulous care.

8. Eines der beiden Schlafzimmer. Die Glasschiebetüren haben Aluminiumrahmen und Vorhänge aus Holzstabgewebe. Hinter der schachbrettartig gemusterten Schrankwand, deren Felder aus Japanpapier bestehen, liegt das zweite Schlafzimmer. Die Kinder rollen ihre Betten abends an einen selbstgewählten Platz.
9. Ostbalkon mit Eßplatz. Alle Details der Konstruktion sind mit besonderer Sorgfalt ausgeführt.

Summer house in the Island of Bornholm

Architects: Gunnar Jensen and Finn Monies, Copenhagen

This cottage stands on an exposed part of the island's rocky coast. It was necessary, therefore not only to build economically but also to adopt a building method solid enough to withstand weather and wind. In addition the architect desired to interfere as little as possible with the landscape and vegetation. A light timber structure with slim posts and beams was chosen, constructed with particularly meticulous workmanship on three concrete strip foundations. The twin beams of the floor deck, which is raised above ground, as well as the posts inserted and bolted to it and the roof joists are dark-stained and provide an effective contrast to the untreated deal facing of the outer walls. Floor and ceilings are likewise of untreated deal. Only the central core with kitchen, bathroom and fireplace is built in brick, and white-washed.

Sommerhaus auf der Insel Bornholm

Architekten: Gunnar Jensen und Finn Monies, Kopenhagen

Dieses Sommer-Ferienhaus liegt exponiert an der Steilküste der Insel. Deshalb mußte nicht nur eine wirtschaftliche, sondern auch eine besonders solide Bauweise gewählt werden, die Wind und Wetter standhält; außerdem waren das Landschaftsbild und die Vegetation möglichst wenig anzutasten. Man entschied sich für eine leichte Holzkonstruktion mit schlank dimensionierten Pfosten und Balken, die mit größter handwerklicher Sorgfalt über drei Beton-Streifenfundamenten errichtet wurde. Die Doppelbalken der vom Boden abgehobenen Bodenplatte, die darin eingezapften und verschraubten Stützpfosten und das Dachgebälk wurden schwarz gebeizt und heben sich wirkungsvoll von der naturfarbenen Tannenholzverschalung der Außenwände ab. Nur der Installationskern mit Bad und Kamin wurde gemauert und weiß gestrichen.

1. View from the east. The sloping ground is compensated for by the concrete strip foundations.

2. Cross-sections. Key: 1 Corrugated asbestos cement roofing 2 Purlins, 3 Rockwool mats, 4 Felting, 5 Ceiling, 6 Rafters, 7 Timber post, 8 Timber joist, 9 Fascia board, 10 Wall cladding, 11 Light-weight panel, 12 Plastic laminate, 13 White-washed foundation, 14 Wooden floor, 15 Framing, 16 Insertion boards, 17 Joist frame.

3. Plan. Key: 1 Entrance and hall, 2 Kitchen, 3 Dining area, 4 Covered terrace, 5 Living room, 6 Master bedroom, 7 Children's and guest room, 8 Bathroom.

4. Living room, with the fireplace of whitewashed brick. Posts and roof joists are dark-stained. Ceiling and floors are of untreated deal. Wall units faced with white plastic laminate panels.

1. Gesamtansicht von Osten. Die Streifenfundamente aus Beton gleichen die Bodenwellen aus.

2. Querschnitt. Legende: 1 Dachdeckung aus Welleternit, 2 Pfetten, 3 Steinwollmatten, 4 Pappenlage, 5 Deckenschalung, 6 Sparren, 7 Holzstütze, 8 Holzriegel, 9 Stirnbrett, 10 Wandschalung, 11 Leichtbauplatte, 12 Novopan, 13 Fundament weißgekälkt, 14 Holzfußboden, 15 Rahmenschenkel, 16 Einschubbretter, 17 Balkenlage.

3. Grundriß. Legende: 1 Eingang und Diele, 2 Küche, 3 Eßplatz, 4 überdachte Terrasse, 5 Wohnraum, 6 Elternschlafzimmer, 7 Kinder- und Gastzimmer, 8 Bad.

4. Der Wohnraum mit dem gemauerten, weiß gestrichenen Kamin. Stütz- und Deckenbalken schwarz gebeizt. Decke und Boden in naturfarbenem Fichtenholz. Wandteile mit weißen Novopanplatten verkleidet.

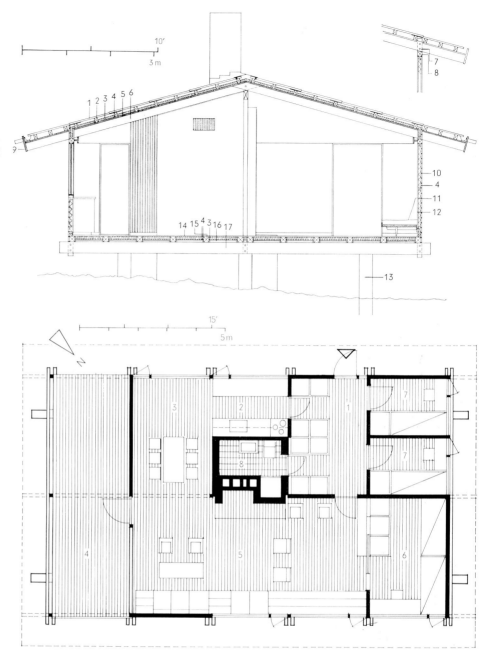

5. North-east side, seen from the beach. Orientation and plan of the house are governed by the sea view.

6. West side (off-shore side). The roof is covered by grey asbestos cement slabs.

7, 8. The lightness of the structure and the slenderness of the posts are particularly apparent at the west-side terrace.

9. The north-east windows of the living room offer a wide sea view. The view on the coast offered by the full-height windows on the south-east side is hardly impeded by the unobtrusive railing of the terrace.

10. Dining corner and kitchen are directly adjacent; the passage can be closed by a sliding door.

5. Die Nordostseite vom Strand aus gesehen. Orientierung und Raumaufteilung des Hauses sind durch die Aussicht auf die Ostsee und Küste bedingt.

6. Blick von Westen auf die Landseite mit dem Eingang. Das Dach ist mit grauen Welleternitplatten gedeckt.

7, 8. Die Leichtigkeit der Konstruktion und die schlanken Abmessungen der Stützen treten bei der Terrasse auf der Westseite besonders deutlich in Erscheinung.

9. Durch die Fenster auf der Nordostseite des Wohnraums bietet sich eine weite Aussicht über die Ostsee. Das leichte Geländer der Terrasse behindert kaum den Blick auf die Küste, den die raumhohe Verglasung der Südostseite freigibt.

10. Eßnische und Küche liegen direkt nebeneinander; der Durchgang kann durch eine Schiebetür geschlossen werden, die in der Wandvertäfelung läuft.

House at Tegernsee

Architect: Hans Busso von Busse, Munich

This house, erected by the architect for his own use, stands on the shore of Tegernsee, less than an hour's car ride from his Munich office. It is therefore designed for frequent use, and more luxuriously equipped than a normal weekend and vacation house. There are no corridors or passages. All the living rooms and bedrooms are linked with the surrounding porch. By removing some sliding doors, the entrance hall can be combined with both living rooms so as to form one large single space. Timber framework placed on a reinforced concrete slab; end bays braced by steel bars. Double and treble section posts of dowelled oak strip into which the wooden rafters are inserted. Ceiling faced with narrow larch wood strip; walls plastered or faced with yellow bricks; brick flooring; roof covered with special flat pantiles.

Landhaus am Tegernsee

Architekt: Hans Busso von Busse, München

Der Architekt errichtete sein eigenes Haus am Tegernsee, nur eine knappe Autostunde von seiner Münchner Arbeitsstätte entfernt. So ist es auf häufige Benutzung eingerichtet und anspruchsvoller gestaltet als das übliche Wochenend- und Ferienhaus. Eigentliche Verkehrsräume fehlen. Sämtliche Wohn- und Schlafräume öffnen sich nach der umlaufenden Terrasse. Die Eingangshalle kann durch Öffnen von Schiebetüren mit den beiden Wohnräumen zu einem großen Aufenthaltsraum kombiniert werden. Holzskelettkonstruktion auf Stahlbetonplatte: Zwillings- und Drillingsstützen aus miteinander verdübelten Eichenholzprofilen mit eingeschobenen Sparrenholzbindern. Deckenverschalung aus schmalen Lärchenholzriemen, Wände weiß verputzt oder mit gelbem Klinker vermauert; Klinkerfußboden. Kaltdach mit Spezialflachdachpfannen gedeckt.

1. South side, with the covered porch outside the living room. On the left, passage to the conservatory.
2. East side. Each living and bedroom has direct access to the surrounding porch.
3. Section of house and conservatory, with open passage.
4. Plan. Key: 1 Entrance hall and dining area, 2 Kitchen, 3 Small sitting room, 4 Bedroom, 5 Large sitting room with fireplace, 6 Study, 7 Covered terrace, 8 Bathroom, 9 Greenhouse workroom, 10 Conservatory.
5. Night view through the porch into the large sitting room with the fireplace.

1. Ansicht von Süden mit dem gedeckten Sitzplatz vor dem Wohnraum. Links der Durchgang zum Gewächshaus.
2. Längsseite von Osten. Jeder Wohn- und Schlafraum hat einen direkten Ausgang auf die umlaufende Terrasse.
3. Querschnitt durch Wohnhaus und Gewächshaus mit Verbindungsgang.
4. Grundriß. Legende: 1 Eingangshalle mit Eßplatz, 2 Küche, 3 kleiner Wohnraum, 4 Schlafraum, 5 großer Wohnraum mit Kamin, 6 Arbeitsraum, 7 gedeckte Terrasse, 8 Bad, 9 Arbeitsraum im Gewächshaus, 10 Gewächshaus.
5. Blick über die umlaufende Terrasse in den großen Wohnraum mit Kamin.

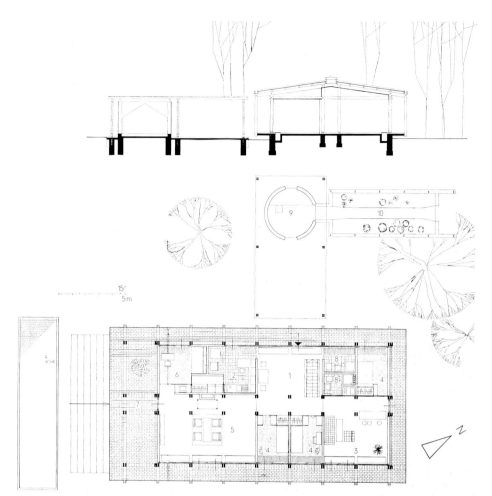

6. Part of south side, with the porch which surrounds the entire house, serving as passage. The end bays of the timber structure are braced by steel bar ties. A slackenning of the ties can be compensated, i.e. retensioned with spanners.
7. From the smaller sitting room, sliding doors give access to bathroom and WC.
8. Part of living room, with fireplace.
9. View from the small sitting room towards the dining area at the entrance.
10. The smaller sitting room, with bar and false ceiling.
11. Dining area at the entrance, with the two east facing bedrooms in the background. On the right the passage to the larger living room, on the left the door of the small sitting room.

6. Ausschnitt aus der Südseite mit der gedeckten Terrasse, die als Laufgang um das ganze Haus weitergeführt ist. In den Endfeldern steifen Zugstäbe aus Rundstahl die Holzkonstruktion aus. Das Erlahmen der Zugstäbe kann durch Nachspannen von Spannschlössern ausgeglichen werden.
7. Vom kleinen Wohnraum aus sind Bad und WC durch Schiebetüren zugänglich.
8. Detail aus dem Wohnraum mit Kamin.
9. Blick aus dem kleinen Wohnraum auf die Diele mit Eßplatz.
10. Kleiner Wohnraum mit Bar und eingezogener Lamellendecke.
11. Eßplatz in der Eingangsdiele mit Blick auf die beiden Schlafräume an der Ostseite. Rechts der Durchgang zum großen Wohnraum, links die Tür des kleinen Wohnzimmers.

House on Cap Bénat (Côte d'Azur)

Architects: André Lefèvre and Jean Aubert, Le Lavandou, Var

This single-room house (Type C) is part of a resort village on Cap Bénat on the French Riviera. The architects tried to integrate the buildings as unobtrusively as possible with the surrounding rock and pinewood landscape. The different houses were therefore built of local stone, and the flat roofs treated as gardens, almost indistinguishable from the hillside. To preserve the integrity of the entire village, the individual houses are largely standardised. Strong stone walls ensure privacy and provide protection against mistral and wind from the sea. To each house belongs a small garden and open terrace with a sea view. All the external woodwork is untreated. The flooring inside the houses is of terracotta.

Ferienhaus auf dem Cap Bénat (Côte d'Azur)

Architekten: André Lefèvre und Jean Aubert, Le Lavandou/Var

Das Einraumhaus (Typ C) gehört zu einem auf dem Cap Bénat an der Côte d'Azur erbauten Feriendorf. Es kam den Architekten darauf an, die Bauten möglichst unauffällig in die Landschaft mit ihren Felsen und Pinienwäldern einzugliedern. Aus diesem Grund verwendeten sie zum Bau der verschiedenen Haustypen den örtlichen Naturstein und bepflanzten die flachen Dächer, so daß sie von oben gesehen wie hängende Gärten erscheinen. Die einzelnen Ferienhäuser sind mit Rücksicht auf die Einheitlichkeit der Gesamtanlage weitgehend genormt. Kräftige Steinmauern schirmen sie gegen den Mistral und den Wind vom Meer sowie gegen Einsicht vom Nachbargrundstück her ab. Zu jedem Haus gehört ein kleiner Garten und eine offene Terrasse mit Blick auf das Meer. Sämtliche Holzteile der Außenkonstruktion sind naturfarben. Der Fußboden im Inneren besteht aus Terrakotta.

1. House, Type C. Walls, stairs and balustrades are of local stone and uniform appearance.
2. The village, surrounded by pinewoods, facing the sea.
3. View on the flat roofs, showing the roof gardens in various stages of development. On some houses, the patios are covered by pergolas where straw mats can be fixed as a sun protection.
4, 5. House, Type C. Plan and south-east elevation. Key: 1 Access, 2 Sitting corner, 3 Dining area, 4 Kitchenette, 5 Shower bath, 6 Washroom with WC, 7 Bedroom, 8 Open terrace.
6. Corner of the house, with wooden folding door affording sun protection to the living room.

1. Ferienhaus Typ C. Wände und Gartenmauern einheitlich aus örtlichem Naturstein.
2. Das Feriendorf umgeben von Pinienwäldern mit dem Blick auf das Meer.
3. Blick auf die flachen Dächer mit den Dachgärten in verschiedenen Stadien der Bepflanzung. Bei einzelnen Häusern sind die Gartenhöfe von Pergolen überspannt, unter deren Balken Strohmatten als Sonnenschutz befestigt werden können.
4, 5. Ferienhaus Typ C. Grundriß und Ansicht von Südosten. Legende: 1 Zugang, 2 Sitzecke, 3 Eßplatz, 4 Kochnische, 5 Dusche, 6 Waschraum mit WC, 7 Schlafteil, 8 offene Terrasse.
6. Hausecke mit Holzfalttür als Sonnenschutz vor dem Wohnraum.

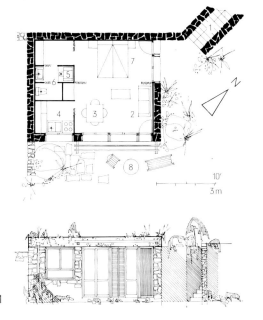

House at Lake Sempach

Architect: Robert Hofer, Zurich

The east side of this house, designed for a family with three children on a small area of approximately 26×26 ft, faces Lake Sempach. Towards the south, there is a magnificent view of the mountain world of Pilatus and Rigi. The house, constructed of timber, has a single room surrounded by a narrow porch. So that the reeds surrounding the lake should not impair the view, the house was raised on a platform supported by concrete piers. By means of folding partitions, the room can be divided into sleeping cabins at night. One partition is extended from the east wall and another from the south wall to the fireplace, creating two small cabins with one bed each. Above each of these beds, another bed can be swung out which, in daytime, is hidden in the wall. In the north-west corner are kitchenette, a shower bath with WC, and a small storeroom.

Wochenend- und Ferienhaus am Sempacher See

Architekt: Robert Hofer, Zürich

Die Ostseite dieses auf einer Grundfläche von knapp 8×8 m besonders raumsparend eingerichteten Wochenend- und Ferienhauses für eine Familie mit drei Kindern geht auf den Sempacher See. Nach Süden bietet sich eine prächtige Aussicht auf die Bergwelt von Pilatus und Rigi. Es wurde als Einraum aus Holz erstellt und hat eine schmale umlaufende Terrasse. Um zu verhindern, daß der Schilfgürtel am Seeufer die Aussicht behinderte, wurde es durch ein Podest auf Betonsockeln vom Boden abgehoben. Durch Faltwände läßt sich der Wohnraum nachts in Schlafkojen aufteilen. Aus der Ost- und Südwand wird je eine mobile Wand bis zum Kamin aufgefaltet, so daß zwei kleine Kojen mit je einem Bett entstehen. Über diese Betten wird je ein weiteres Bett heruntergeklappt, das tagsüber in die Wand versenkt ist. An der Nordwestecke befinden sich die Kochnische, die Dusche mit WC und ein Abstellraum.

1. East side of the house, facing the lake, with the wooden wall panel and the full-height glass sliding panels.
2. East side with the panels opened.
3. South side.
4. Plan. Key: By day: 1+2+3 Living room; by night: 1 Master bedroom, 2 Children's bedroom, 3 Children's bedroom, 4 Surrounding porch, 5 Changing cabin, 6 Kitchenette, 7 Shower bath and WC, 8 Store room; the broken lines indicate the position of the folding partitions.

1. Blick vom See her auf die Ostseite mit der feststehenden Holzwand und den raumhohen Glasschiebetüren.
2. Die Ostseite bei geöffneten Türen.
3. Die Südseite.
4. Grundriß. Legende: tagsüber 1+2+3 Wohnraum; nachts 1 Elternschlafraum, 2 Kinderschlafraum, 3 Kinderschlafraum, 4 Terrasse, 5 Umkleidekabine, 6 Kochnische, 7 Dusche und WC, 8 Abstellraum. Gestrichelte Linien: Faltwände.

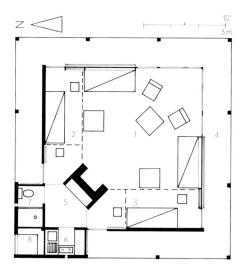

5. Interior by day. One of the tip-up beds can be seen on the north wall, above the picture. To the left of it is a folding partition in the folded position.
6. Interior by night. The folding partitions separating the children's sleeping bunks are closed.

5. Blick ins Innere bei Tag. In der Nordwand ist über dem Bild eines der versenkten Klappbetten zu erkennen; links davon eine zusammengeschobene Faltwand.
6. Der Innenraum in Nachtstellung. Die Faltwände vor den Schlafkojen der Kinder sind geschlossen.

Cottage on a Finnish Island

Architects: Keijo Ström and Olavi Tuomisto, Helsinki

This house stands on the narrowest point, no wider than 50 ft, of a reef about one-third of a mile long. On concrete posts adapted to the sloping site, rests a platform which carries a timber structure with 5×10 cm posts, conforming to a module of 60 cm. The structure is faced with white-painted boarding outside. The plan is U-shaped, open to the west. A central, partially covered terrace is flanked on the south and east sides by living room, bedroom, dining area and kitchen and, on the north side, by the sauna. Access is by wooden stairs which extend the whole width of the jetty. The open and semi-open terraces occupy nearly half the area of the plan; with the sloping roof which dominates the west side, they represent the most notable features of this house.

Ferienhaus auf einer finnischen Felseninsel

Architekten: Keijo Ström und Olavi Tuomisto, Helsinki

Das Ferienhaus steht auf der schmalsten Stelle einer 600 m langen, hier nur knapp 15 m breiten Felseninsel. Auf Betonpfeilern, die dem Gelände angepaßt sind, ruht eine Plattform, auf der über einem Rastermodul von 60 cm eine Skelettkonstruktion aus Holzstützen von 5×10 cm errichtet wurde. Sie ist außen mit weiß gestrichenen Holzbrettern abgedeckt. Das Haus ist auf U-förmigem Grundriß nach Westen orientiert, wobei sich Aufenthaltsraum, Schlafteil und Eßplatz mit anschließender Küche und der Nordflügel mit der Sauna um eine zentral gelegene, teilweise überdeckte Terrasse gruppieren. Man betritt das Haus vom Landungssteg her über eine Holztreppe in der vollen Breite des Stegs. Die offenen und halboffenen Außenräume nehmen fast die Hälfte des Grundrisses ein und geben zusammen mit dem Pultdach, das die Höhe der Westfront betont, dem Ferienhaus sein charakteristisches Gepräge.

1. West side with the main entrance, reached from the jetty by a broad flight of stairs. Behind the white-painted latticework on the left, designed to ensure privacy, is the sauna terrace and sauna.
2. Jetty and house are integrated by the full-width steps. The jetty itself, also painted white, is used as another outdoor sitting area. The steps lead to the central terrace.
3. Flanking the central terrace on the south side is a broad veranda outside the glass-fronted living room.
4. West elevation.
5. Plan. Key: 1 Living room, 2 Sleeping bunks, 3 Dining corner, 4 Kitchen, 5 Stores, 6 Covered dining terrace, 7 Terrace, 8 Sauna terrace, 9 Changing room, 10 Sauna, 11 Stairs, 12 Jetty.
6. South elevation and sections.

1. Die nach Westen orientierte Hauptfront mit dem Landungssteg und der breiten Treppe. Hinter den weiß gestrichenen Sichtschutzblenden links liegen Saunaterrasse und Sauna.
2. Landungssteg und Haus sind durch eine Treppe in der Breite des Stegs zu einer Einheit verbunden. Der ebenfalls weiß gestrichene Steg wird als zusätzlicher Freisitzplatz verwendet. Die Treppe führt auf die zentrale Terrasse.
3. An die zentrale Terrasse schließt sich im Süden eine breite Veranda an, die dem verglasten Wohnraum vorgelagert ist.
4. Ansicht von Westen.
5. Grundriß. Legende: 1 Wohnraum, 2 Schlafplätze, 3 Eßecke, 4 Küche, 5 Vorräte, 6 gedeckte Eßterrasse, 7 Terrasse, 8 Saunaterrasse, 9 Umkleideraum, 10 Sauna, 11 Treppe, 12 Landungssteg.
6. Ansicht von Süden und Querschnitte.

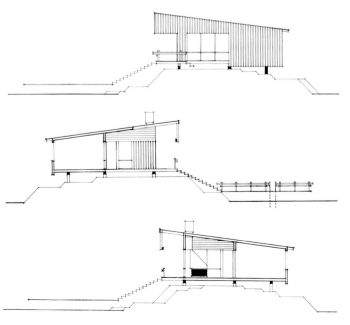

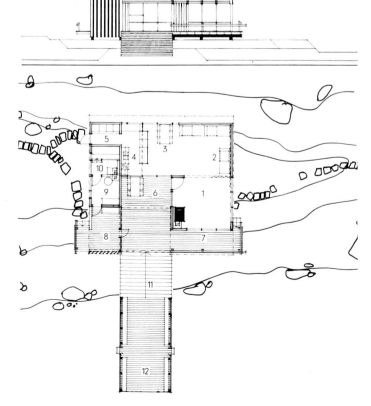

7. South side. On this side, too, the living room has a high window.
8. View from the living room towards south. The islet is so narrow that both banks are visible.
9. The open door leads from the living room to the central dining terrace. In the foreground on the left is the open fireplace.
10. View from the dining area near the kitchen through the window of the central terrace into the living room.
11. View from the central dining terrace towards the dining area near the kitchen.
12. Central terrace with the outdoor dining area.
13. Hatch from the kitchen to the outdoor dining area.

7. Ansicht von Süden. Auch nach dieser Seite hat der Wohnraum ein hohes Fenster.
8. Blick aus dem Wohnraum nach Süden. Die Insel ist so schmal, daß beide Ufer sichtbar sind.
9. Die geöffnete Tür führt aus dem Wohnraum auf die zentrale Eßterrasse. Links im Vordergrund der offene Kamin.
10. Blick vom Eßplatz neben der Küche durch das Fenster der zentralen Terrasse in den Wohnraum.
11. Blick von der zentralen Eßterrasse auf den Eßplatz.
12. Die zentrale Terrasse mit dem Eßplatz im Freien.
13. Durchreiche von der Küche zum Eßplatz auf der Terrasse.

House at Espoo near Helsinki

Architect: Erkii Kairamo, Helsinki

This house stands on a small island near Helsinki which is connected with the shore by a narrow, swampy tongue of land. The L-shaped site faces south and west, and the house itself is orientated accordingly. The full-height windows of the living room and the L-shaped terrace in front of it, face both south and west, affording a wide view and allowing the sun to penetrate deeply into the rooms during the day and in the evening. On the north side of the house are dining area and kitchen. The master bedroom is in the north-west corner, separated merely by a man-high cupboard wall and receiving daylight through a continuous strip of top lighting. A separate sleeping cabin and the sauna are on the east side. The house has a thermal insulation of rockwool slabs and can also be used during the winter.

Ferienhaus in Espoo bei Helsinki

Architekt: Erkii Kairamo, Helsinki

Das Ferienhaus steht in der Nähe von Helsinki auf einer Insel, die durch eine schmale, sumpfige Landzunge mit dem Festland verbunden ist. Das Grundstück hat die Form eines sich nach Süden und Westen hin öffnenden Winkels, dem die Orientierung des Hauses angepaßt ist: Die raumhohen Fenster des Aufenthaltsraums und die L-förmige vorgelagerte Terrasse gehen ebenfalls nach Süden und Westen, so daß man von hier aus einen freien Blick hat und die Tages- und Abendsonne tief in den Raum eindringen kann. Auf der Nordseite des Hauses schließen sich Eßplatz und Küche an. Der Schlafraum der Eltern in der Nordwestecke ist nur durch eine mannshohe Schrankwand abgeteilt. Eine separate Schlafkammer und die Sauna befinden sich auf der Ostseite. Das Haus ist mit Steinwollplatten isoliert und kann auch im Winter benutzt werden.

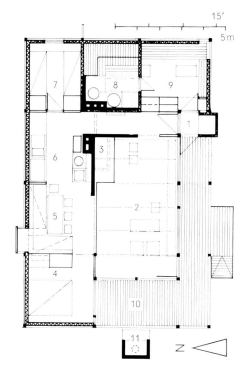

1. West side of the house.
2. Plan. Key: 1 Entrance and porch, 2 Living room, 3 Fireplace, 4 Master bedroom, 5 Dining area, 6 Kitchen, 7 Small bedroom, 8 Sauna, 9 Outer room of sauna, 10 Terrace, 11 Outdoor fireplace.
3. South-west corner with the outdoor fireplace which is served from the L-shaped terrace. Because of the damp ground, the timber structure is raised above ground by means of timber beams.
4. View from the east into the sitting room which is on a lower level. The entire room, with the exception of the small bedroom and the sauna, is heated by an oil stove.
5. North-east corner of living room. The fireplace wall echoes the angle motive on which the entire design is based.

1. Das Haus von Westen.
2. Grundriß. Legende: 1 Eingang und Windfang, 2 Aufenthaltsraum, 3 Kamin, 4 Elternschlafraum, 5 Eßplatz, 6 Küche, 7 Schlafkammer, 8 Sauna, 9 Vorraum zur Sauna, 10 Terrasse, 11 Außenkamin.
3. Die Südwestecke mit dem Außenkamin, der von der L-förmigen Terrasse aus beheizt wird. Die Holzkonstruktion ist des feuchten Untergrundes wegen auf Holzbalken vom Terrain abgesetzt.
4. Blick von Osten in den tiefer liegenden Aufenthaltsraum. Als Wärmequelle dient ein Ölkamin, der den Gesamtraum mit Ausnahme der Schlafkammer und der Sauna beheizt. Die Bänke am Eßplatz dienen ebenfalls als Betten.
5. Nordostecke des Aufenthaltsraumes. Die Kaminwand (vor der Küche) nimmt das Winkelmotiv auf, das dem Entwurf zugrunde liegt.

House at Teisko, Finland

Architects: Mirja and Heikki Castrén,
Helsinki

This house stands on a rocky plateau but takes shelter in a small depression in a wooded setting. The east-to-west wing of the house (which is L-shaped) is taken up by the living-cum-dining room which is covered by a lean-to-roof rising, on the south side, to nearly twice the height of the room. In the north-to-south wing are the master bedroom and two smaller bedrooms; kitchen, bathroom and WC are placed at the intersection of both wings. The triangular end walls of the living room wing reach out northwards and provide a frame for the terrace outside. The roof rafters inside remain visible and, with the spruce wood facing of ceiling and walls, give the room its character. The landscape is brought into the house through the full-height glass windows on the two long sides of the living room which has, under the hood of the roof, a remarkable transparency.

Ferienhaus in Teisko, Finnland

Architekten: Mirja und Heikki Castrén,
Helsinki

Das auf dem Felsplateau einer Bergkuppe errichtete Haus schmiegt sich zwischen lockerem Baumbestand in eine Mulde. Der Ostwestflügel des L-förmigen Gebäudes wird von dem kombinierten Wohn- und Eßraum eingenommen, dessen Pultdach nach Süden auf nahezu doppelte Raumhöhe ansteigt. Im Nordsüdflügel sind der Elternschlafraum und zwei kleinere Schlafräume untergebracht, während Küche und Installationszelle im Schnittpunkt der beiden Trakte liegen. Die dreieckigen Giebelwände des Wohnteils greifen nach Norden aus und rahmen die vorgelagerte Terrasse ein. Im Inneren sind die Dachbalken sichtbar belassen und bestimmen mit der Tannenholzschalung von Decke und Wand den Charakter des Raumes. Durch wandhohe Glasfenster ist die Landschaft in das Haus hereingeholt, zugleich bekommt der Wohnflügel eine überraschende Transparenz.

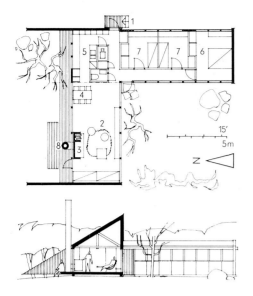

1. Living room, facing west wall.
2. Plan and section. Key: 1 Entrance,
2 Sitting room, 3 Fireplace, 4 Dining area,
5 Kitchen, 6 Master bedroom, 7 Bedroom,
8 Terrace.
3. Kitchen and passage to the bedroom
wing can be closed by sliding doors.
4. South side of living room wing.
5. North side, with the freestanding chimney.

1. Wohnraum mit westlichem Giebel.
2. Grundriß und Schnitt. Legende: 1 Eingang, 2 Wohnraum, 3 Kamin, 4 Eßplatz,
5 Küche, 6 Elternschlafraum, 7 Schlafraum, 8 Terrasse.
3. West-Ost- Blick durch den Wohnraum.
4. Wohntrakt-Südseite mit Eternitplatten.
5. Gesamtansicht von Norden.

**House on the Golfe de Trayas
(French Riviera)**

Architect: Marcel Gogois, Cannes

The house is situated on a cliff jutting out into the Mediterranean. It was therefore obvious that the terraces and patio on the south and east sides had to be opened up towards the sea. This has been made easier by the structural design, with overhanging tee trusses of timber freely spanning the outdoor sitting area on the south side. The interior has a L-shaped plan, with the living room and sleeping bunks forming a large coherent space on the east side. Two steps lead from the living room to the square part on the northwest side, containing kitchen, bathroom and an additional bedroom. Base and north wall are of rubble walling; the timber structure is covered with reddish pinewood boards. The overhanging tiled roof provides shade for the windows of the living room which is deliberately designed as a place of rest and is therefore not directly connected with the patio.

**Ferienhaus am Golfe de Trayas
(Côte d'Azur)**

Architekt: Marcel Gogois, Cannes

Die Lage auf einem Felsvorsprung legte es nahe, das Haus auf der Süd- und Ostseite mit Terrassen und Patio zum Meer hin auszurichten. Diesem Öffnen des Baukörpers kam die Konstruktion aus T-förmigen Holzbindern entgegen, deren Kragarme auf der Südseite geschützte Freisitzplätze stützenfrei überspannen. Der innere Wohnteil hat einen L-förmigen Grundriß, wobei Wohnraum und Schlafkoje als großer, zusammenhängender Raum auf die Ostseite gelegt wurden. Zwei Stufen führen vom Wohnraum in den quadratischen Nordwestteil mit Küche, Bad und zusätzlichem Schlafraum. Sockel und Nordwand bestehen aus Naturstein, die Holzkonstruktion wurde mit rötlichen Kiefernholzdielen verschalt. Das mit Ziegeln gedeckte Kragdach beschattet die Fenster des Wohnraumes, der als Zone der Ruhe nicht direkt an den Patio angeschlossen ist.

1. South-east side of the house which is situated high above the bay at the edge of a pinewood.
2. The patio, facing south-west, has a covering of reed mats. The rafters avoid the pinetree which was left standing.
3. Plan. Key: 1 Entrance, 2 Patio, 3 Hall, 4 Living room, 5 Sleeping bunk, 6 Kitchen, 7 Bathroom, 8 WC, 9 Bedroom with two-tier beds, 10 Covered terrace.
4. South side. Outdoor sitting area, protected by the tee trusses. On the left the patio, on the right the south terrace. The divan bed is occasionally used as an outdoor spare bed.

1. Blick von Südosten auf das hoch über der Bucht am Rande eines Pinienwaldes gelegene Haus.
2. Der nach Südwesten gelegene Patio ist nur mit Rohrmatten abgedeckt. Die Dachpfetten wurden um die stehengebliebene Pinie herumgeführt.
3. Grundriß. Legende: 1 Eingang, 2 Patio, 3 Eingangshalle, 4 Wohnraum, 5 Schlafkoje, 6 Küche, 7 Bad, 8 WC, 9 Schlafraum mit Doppelstockbetten, 10 überdeckte Terrasse.
4. Südseite. Freiräume unter T-förmigen Dachbindern: links der Patio, rechts die Südterrasse. Das Sofa wird gelegentlich auch als Gästebett im Freien benutzt.

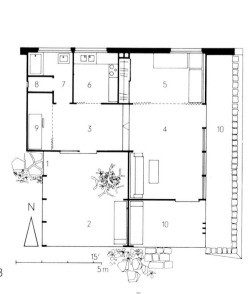

Cottage on Martha's Vineyard Island, Massachusetts

Architect: Eliot Noyes, New Canaan, Connecticut

This island cottage, which the architect built for his own use, stands isolated between shrubs and low pines and affords a view both of the sea and a small fishing village. The family and their guests spend their time here in complete informality, swimming, fishing and sailing. In keeping with this purpose, the house (which can accommodate up to ten people) is designed and furnished for simplicity and comfort. It looks almost like a square shed and consists of a timber structure with cypress wood cladding on the outside. The sloping roof also covers an open porch which is separated by a glass wall from the living room, dining area and kitchen unit. Because of the comparatively steep slope of the roof, it has been possible to provide a gallery floor in the rear of the house, containing two bedrooms with four bunk beds, and a bathroom.

Ferienhaus auf der Insel Martha's Vineyard in Massachusetts

Architekt: Eliot Noyes, New Canaan, Connecticut

Das Sommerhaus, das sich der Architekt auf einer Insel erbaute, liegt zwischen Buschwerk und niedrigen Nadelbäumen mit Blick auf das Meer und ein kleines Fischerdorf. Die Familie verbringt hier mit ihren Gästen die Ferien in völliger Ungezwungenheit beim Baden, Fischen und Segeln. Dementsprechend sind Anlage und Einrichtung des Hauses, das bis zu zehn Personen aufnehmen kann, auf Einfachheit und Bequemlichkeit abgestimmt. Es wirkt wie ein annähernd quadratischer Schuppen und besteht aus einer Holzkonstruktion, die außen mit Zypressenholz verschalt wurde. Das Pultdach ist über eine offene Veranda heruntergezogen, an die – durch eine Glaswand getrennt – Wohnraum, Eßplatz und Küchenblock anschließen. Der verhältnismäßig steile Anstieg des Daches erlaubte es, zwei Schlafräume mit acht Betten und einem Bad auf eine Galerie zu verlegen.

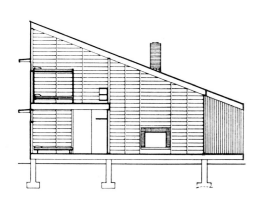

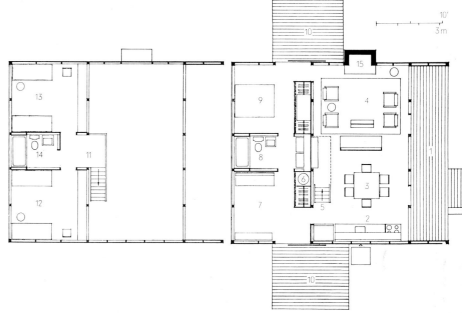

1. In front of the house is a deep porch, protected by the sloping roof.

2. Section, gallery floor plan and ground floor plan. Key: 1 Porch, 2 Kitchen, 3 Dining area, 4 Fireside sitting area, 5 Stairs leading to gallery, 6 Hotwater boiler, 7 Lumber room and playroom, 8 Bathroom, 9 Master bedroom, 10 Outdoor sitting space, 11 Landing, 12 Boys' bedroom, 13 Girls' bedroom, 14 Bathroom, 15 Fireplace.

3. Inside the house, ceiling, walls and floors are covered with red spruce. In addition to the open fireplace, a hotwater heating system is provided. On the left, the gallery floor.

4. Side view. The wooden sliding door leads to a hall which is used for keeping sports equipment and as a playroom. The cypress cladding has not been stained and has assumed a greyish colour naturally.

1. Der Glaswand der Vorderfront ist eine breite Veranda vorgelagert, über die das Pultdach heruntergezogen ist.

2. Schnitt, Grundriß des Galeriegeschosses und des Erdgeschosses. Legende: 1 Veranda, 2 Küchenbereich, 3 Eßplatz, 4 Sitzgruppe mit Kamin, 5 Treppe zum Galeriegeschoß, 6 Warmwasserboiler, 7 Abstell- und Spielraum, 8 Bad, 9 Elternschlafraum, 10 Freisitzplatz, 11 Galerie, 12 Bubenschlafraum, 13 Mädchenschlafraum, 14 Bad, 15 Kamin.

3. Decke, Wände und Fußboden des Innenraums sind mit Rottanne verschalt. Außer dem offenen Kamin ist eine Warmwasserheizung vorgesehen. Links oben das Galeriegeschoß.

4. Seitenansicht. Die Holzschiebetür führt in die Eingangsdiele, die als Abstellraum für Sportgeräte und als Spielzimmer benutzt wird. Die Zypressenholzverschalung wurde nicht imprägniert und hat eine zartgraue Farbe angenommen.

House near San Francisco, California

Architects: Robert B. Marquis and Claude
Stoller, San Francisco

This house, designed for a family of six, stands on a hillside overlooking a lagoon to the north of San Francisco, offering a splendid view up to the town. With its hexagonal shape and sloping roof, it gives the appearance of a tent; this applies, in particular, to the interior which basically consists of a single room only. An open gallery floor serves as a dormitory; below it is the kitchen, bathroom, a store room and the fireplace recess. Kitchen and fireplace open up towards the living room which takes up more than half the interior space. The timber framework has a plywood skin on the inside, and one of red spruce boarding on the outside. The diagonally arranged roof shingles are placed on exposed rafters which rest on a plywood box girder serving as a ridge beam. Floors are partly of deal, partly of concrete.

**Ferienhaus bei San Francisco,
Kalifornien**

Architekten: Robert B. Marquis und Claude Stoller, San Francisco

Dieses Ferienhaus, das für eine Familie mit vier Kindern erbaut wurde, liegt auf einer Anhöhe über einer Lagune nördlich von San Francisco und bietet eine prachtvolle Aussicht bis hinüber zur Stadt. Durch seine sechseckige Form und das Satteldach wirkt es wie ein Zelt, besonders im Inneren, das eigentlich nur aus einem einzigen Raum besteht. Ein offenes Galeriegeschoß wird zum Schlafen benutzt, darunter liegen Küche, Bad, Vorratsraum und Kaminnische. Küche und Kaminecke sind zum Wohnraum hin, der über die Hälfte der Grundfläche einnimmt, offen. Die Konstruktion besteht aus einem Holzskelett, das innen mit Sperrholzplatten verkleidet und außen mit Rotholzbrettern horizontal verschalt ist. Für das Dach sind diagonal verlaufende Schalbretter auf sichtbaren Sparren verwendet, die auf einem Sperrholz-Kastenträger als Firstbalken aufliegen. Der Fußboden besteht aus Fichtenholzdielen und Beton.

1. West side. The timber bridge provides a direct entrance to the bedrooms on the gallery floor. The terrace on the right resumes the hexagonal theme.

2. Section and ground floor plan. Key: 1 Entrance, 2 Living room, 3 Kitchen, 4 Fireplace recess, 5 Utility room, 6 Bathroom and WC, 7 Stairs leading to gallery floor, 8 Bridge leading to gallery floor, 9 Terrace.

3. East side, with the large sliding windows of the living room and the surrounding terrace which, like the bridge leading to the gallery floor, is in keeping with the hexagonal plan.

4. South-west side. The chimney base is protected by hexagonal drainage tiles.

5. South side. The terrace is raised above the ground by a timber structure.

1. Gesamtansicht von Westen. Die Holzbrücke links führt direkt in den Schlafteil im Galeriegeschoß. Die Terrasse nimmt die Sechseckform des Hauses auf.

2. Querschnitt und Grundriß des Erdgeschosses. Legende: 1 Eingang, 2 Wohnraum, 3 Küche, 4 Kaminnische, 5 Vorratsraum, 6 Bad und WC, 7 Treppe zum Obergeschoß, 8 Brücke zum Galeriegeschoß, 9 Terrasse.

3. Die Ostseite mit den großen Schiebefenstern des Wohnraums und dem umlaufenden Balkon, der ebenso wie die Brücke zum Galeriegeschoß dem Sechseckgrundriß angepaßt ist.

4. Die Südwestseite mit der Ummantelung des Kamins aus sechseckigen Drainageziegeln.

5. Ansicht von Süden.

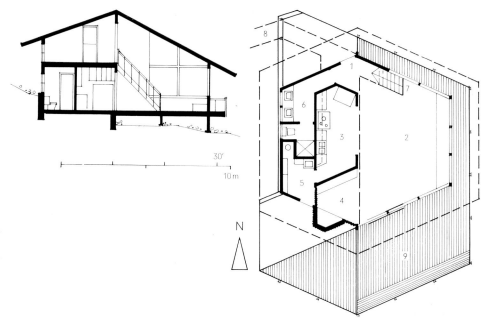

6. A view from the gallery floor into the living room. The built-in window seat on the east side stores foam rubber mattresses which can be used as spare beds.

7. The living room has glass walls on three sides. In the background next to the fireplace recess is the sliding door leading to the south terrace.

8. The wall of the fireside recess is covered with hexagonal terracotta drainage pipes placed vertically.

9. View from the living room towards kitchen recess, entrance and stairs leading to the gallery floor.

6. Blick vom Galeriegeschoß in den Wohnteil. Längs der Ostseite ist eine breite Bank mit Schaumgummimatratzen angebracht, die auch als Schlafgelegenheit für Gäste dient.

7. Der Wohnraum ist auf drei Seiten verglast. Links neben der Kaminnische die Schiebetür zur Südterrasse. Fußboden aus Fichtenholzriemen oder Beton.

8. Die Kaminwand trägt eine Verkleidung aus vertikal gemauerten, sechseckigen Drainageröhren aus Terrakotta.

9. Blick vom Wohnraum auf Küchennische, Eingang und Treppe zum Galeriegeschoß.

Summer weekend house at Upper Wolves Copse, Bosham

Architects: Architects' Co-Partnership, London

This building, situated on the South coast of England near Chichester, was designed for summer weekends or short periods during the holidays. It was therefore possible to keep the construction light. To keep out insects and moisture, and to obtain a free view over the bay, the structure is raised 7 ft off the ground by hardwood posts on concrete foundations. The free space under the living and bedrooms is used as a car park and for storing wood. The house has been constructed entirely of wood and glass and accommodates up to six persons. It comprises a master bedroom with bathroom, a guest bedroom with bathroom, a combined sitting and dining area with the kitchen unit, and a large terrace. The flat roof can be used as an additional sun deck.

Sommer-Wochenendhaus in Upper Wolves Copse, Bosham

Architekten: Architects' Co-Partnership, London

Da dieses Ferienhaus, das an der englischen Kanalküste in der Nähe von Chichester erbaut wurde, nur den Sommer über für Wochenend- und kurze Ferienaufenthalte benutzt wird, konnte die Konstruktion so leicht wie möglich gehalten werden. Um Insekten und Bodenfeuchtigkeit abzuhalten und eine freie Aussicht über die Bucht zu gewinnen, ist der Baukörper auf Hartholzstützen mit Betonsockeln rund 2 m (7 Fuß) vom Terrain abgehoben. Der freie Raum unter den Wohn- und Schlafräumen wird als Wageneinstellplatz und Holzlager benutzt. Das Haus, das ausschließlich aus Holz und Glas besteht, kann bis zu sechs Personen beherbergen. Das Raumprogramm umfaßt ein Schlafzimmer mit Bad für den Hausherrn und ein Gästezimmer mit Bad, ferner den kombinierten Wohn- und Eßraum mit dem Küchenblock sowie ein großes Sonnendeck. Das flache Dach kann als zusätzliche Sonnenterrasse ausgebaut werden.

89

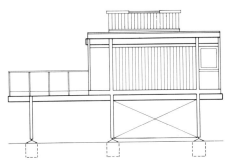

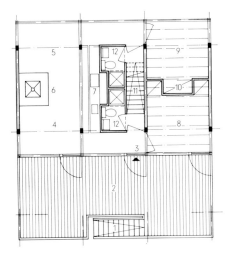

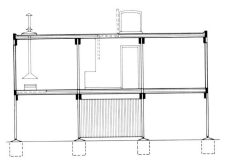

1. (Page 89) General view. At ground level is the walled core with the store room. Access to the main floor is provided by the outdoor stairs leading to the terrace. External elmwood timbering.
2. Covering an area of approximately 30×12 ft, the terrace is not much smaller than the enclosed part of the main floor.
3. Guest room. The box for the bedding under the lower bed can be tipped up.

1. (Seite 89) Gesamtansicht. Im Erdgeschoß der ummauerte Kern mit dem Abstellraum. Zugang zum Obergeschoß über die Außentreppe am Sonnendeck. Außenwände mit Ulmenholz verschalt.
2. Mit 9×3,60 m Fläche ist das Sonnendeck nur wenig kleiner als der umbaute Teil des Wohngeschosses.
3. Gästezimmer. Aufklappbarer Bettzeugkasten unter dem unteren Bett.

4. Longitudinal section, cross-section, upper floor plan, ground floor plan. Key: 1 Stairs leading to upper floor, 2 Terrace, 3 Entrance and hall, 4 Dining area, 5 Living area, 6 Fireplace, 7 Kitchen area, 8 Master bedroom, 9 Guest bedroom, 10 Fitted cupboards, 11 Stairs leading to roof, 12 Shower bath and WC, 13 Car shelter, 14 Store room. The bricked-in part with the store room at ground level is below the sanitary units on the upper floor.

4. Längsschnitt, Querschnitt, Grundrisse des Obergeschosses und des Erdgeschosses. Legende: 1 Treppe zum Obergeschoß, 2 Sonnendeck, 3 Eingang und Diele, 4 Eßplatz, 5 Wohnbereich, 6 Kamin, 7 Küchenblock, 8 Schlafraum des Hausherrn, 9 Gastzimmer, 10 Einbauschränke, 11 Treppe zum Dach, 12 Dusche und WC, 13 Wageneinstellplatz, 14 Abstellraum.

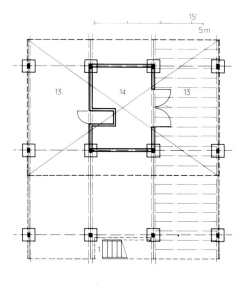

5. View from the dining area towards the open island fireplace and the sitting room chairs. Floors are of maple wood, wall and ceiling lining of pine board. The clerestory windows between the roof joists and the square window sashes at the corners open outwards.

5. Blick vom Eßplatz aus auf den allseitig offenen Kamin und die Sitzgruppe im Wohnbereich. Fußboden aus Ahornriemen, Wände und Decken mit Kiefernholz verschalt. Die Glasstreifen zwischen den Deckenbalken und die quadratischen Fensterflügel werden nach außen geklappt.

6. The service unit forms a compact entity between living room and bedrooms. Behind the fitted kitchen cupboard are two shower bath cabinets, and a WC. On either side are the passages leading to the bedrooms. Some details of the design are borrowed from ship building techniques, eg the stainless steel tie wire bracing to the posts and the sliding roof hatch.

6. Die Naßzelle ist als geschlossener Block zwischen den Wohnraum und die Schlafräume gesetzt. Hinter dem Wandschrank der Küche liegen zwei Duschkabinen mit WC. Rechts und links die Durchgänge zu den Schlafräumen. Einige Details des Hauses stammen aus dem Schiffsbau, so z. B. die Diagonalverspannung aus rostfreien Stahlkabeln zwischen den Erdgeschoßpfosten oder die Schiebetür über der Dachluke.

House near Porvoo, Southern Finland

Architect: Bertel Saarnio, Helsinki

This house, built entirely of timber, is situated close to the Finnish south coast on an untouched site covered with grass, studded with birch and pine trees, and showing outcrops of rock. To obtain the sea view, the house has been raised high above ground on iron-shoed twin timber posts. The living areas and bedrooms are on the upper floor; at ground level, the timber-clad base contains a sauna, dressing room, washroom and the staircase. On the west side of this base is the car shelter and on the east side a covered outdoor seating area with open fireplace. The interior of the upper floor is partitioned into different living room and bedroom areas by cupboard walls and shelves which stop short of the ceiling. Stairs, fireplace and kitchen are combined in the centre of the house.

Ferienhaus bei Porvoo, Südfinnland

Architekt: Bertel Saarnio, Helsinki

Das ganz in Holz konstruierte Ferienhaus steht an der Südküste Finnlands unter hohen Fichten und Birken auf einem grasbewachsenen, mit großen Felsblöcken übersäten Gelände, das unverändert erhalten blieb. Um die Aussicht auf das Meer nicht zu behindern, wurde der Bau auf doppelten Holzstützen mit Eisenfüßen hoch über das Terrain gehoben. Sämtliche Wohn- und Schlafbereiche liegen im Obergeschoß, während in dem holzverschalten Sockel des Untergeschosses eine Sauna mit Ankleide- und Waschraum sowie das Treppenhaus untergebracht sind. Auf der Westseite schließt sich der Wageneinstellplatz und nach Osten zu ein Freisitzplatz mit offenem Kamin an. Der Innenraum des Obergeschosses wird durch Schränke und nicht ganz bis zur Decke reichende Regale in verschiedene Wohn- und Schlafbereiche unterteilt. Treppe, Kaminblock und Kochnische sind im Zentrum des Hauses zusammengefaßt.

1. View from south-west. In the foreground at ground level, the car shelter and behind it the recessed base with staircase and sauna; above it the large living room window. The vertical timber boarding of the upper floor is creosoted; the windows and their surrounds are painted white.
2, 3. South side (top) and north side (offshore side, bottom).
4. Cross-section, with beach.

1. Ansicht von Südwesten. Im Erdgeschoß vorne der Wageneinstellplatz, dahinter der zurückgesetzte Sockel mit Treppenhaus und Sauna, darüber die Fenster des Wohnraums. Die vertikale Holzverschalung des Obergeschosses ist schwarz geteert, übrige Holzteile weiß gestrichen.
2, 3. Gesamtansicht von Süden (oben) und Norden (Rückseite).
4. Schnitt durch das Vorgelände am Meer.

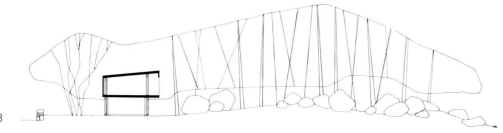

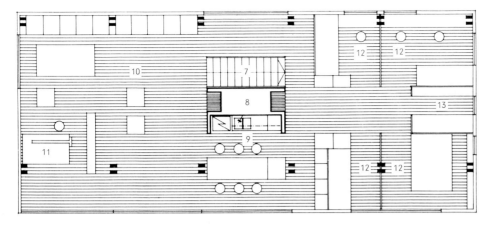

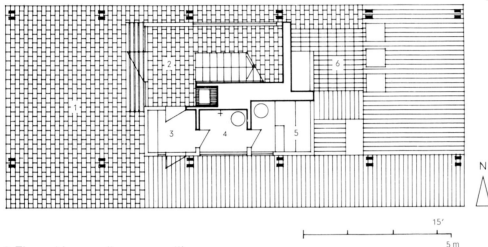

5. Upper floor and ground floor plans. Key: 1 Car shelter, 2 Entrance and staircase, 3 Dressing room, 4 Washroom, 5 Sauna, 6 Outdoor seating area with open fireplace, 7 Stairs, 8 Fireplaces, 9 Kitchen and dining area, 10 Living room area, 11 Study, 12 Bedroom, 13 Cupboard room.

5. Grundrisse Obergeschoß und Untergeschoß. Legende: 1 Wageneinstellplatz, 2 Eingang und Treppenhaus, 3 Ankleideraum, 4 Waschraum, 5 Sauna, 6 Freisitzplatz mit Kamin, 7 Treppe, 8 Kaminblock, 9 Kochnische und Eßplatz, 10 Wohnbereich, 11 Arbeitsplatz, 12 Schlafraum, 13 Schrankraum.

6. The outdoor seating area, with open fireplace, below the eastern part of the house is protected on the north side by wooden blinds. The fireplace surround consists of whitewashed brick.

6. Der Freisitzplatz mit offenem Kamin unter dem Ostteil des Hauses ist nach Norden durch Holzstabvorhänge abgeschirmt. Die Kaminwand wurde aus Backstein gemauert und weiß geschlämmt.

7. North-western corner of the living room with fitted bunks; on the left, the brick surround of the fireplace. Ceiling and floor are unstained timber.
8. View from the dining area across the shelf partition towards the owner's study on the west side.
9. View along the south side living room windows towards the dining area.

7. Die Nordwestecke des Wohnbereichs mit eingebauten Liegebänken, links die gemauerte Kaminwand. Die Holzverschalung von Decke und Fußboden ist natur belassen.
8. Blick vom Eßplatz durch das raumteilende Regal auf die Arbeitsecke des Hausherrn an der Westseite.
9. Blick entlang der verglasten Südfront des Wohnteils auf den Eßplatz.

House at Itaipava near Rio de Janeiro

Architect: Affonso Eduardo Reidy

With its concrete framework and solid brick wall panels, this house, built on a sloping site at an altitude of approximately 2,600 ft in the mountains of Itaipava, forms an impressive contrast to the tropical landscape. The house rests on columns; apart from a spare room with shower bath and WC, the ground floor is left open and serves as a car port. On the main floor, the square floor slab measuring 10×10 metres is of waffle-type construction; six concrete columns in front of the west and east sides carry the two roof vaults. The wall panels are of fair-faced brick, outside and inside. In addition to the living-cum-dining room, the main floor contains a study, a bedroom with shower and WC and the kitchen.

Ferienhaus in Itaipava bei Rio de Janeiro

Architekt: Affonso Eduardo Reidy

Das Wochenendhaus, das in etwa 800 m Höhe im Gebirgsland von Itaipava auf einem Hanggrundstück erbaut wurde, hebt sich mit seiner Betonrahmenkonstruktion und den geschlossenen Wandscheiben aus Backsteinmauerwerk eindrucksvoll von der tropischen Landschaft ab. Der Baukörper steht auf Stützen, wobei das Untergeschoß – abgesehen von einem Gastzimmer mit Dusche und WC – offen gelassen ist und als Wageneinstellplatz dient. Im Wohngeschoß, dessen 10×10 m große Geschoßplatte als Kassettendecke ausgebildet ist, tragen sechs frei vor die West- beziehungsweise Ostfassade gestellte Betonpfeiler zwei tonnenförmig gewölbte Dachschalen. Die Wandfelder sind mit außen und innen sichtbar belassenen, hellen Backsteinen ausgefacht. Das Wohngeschoß umfaßt außer dem Wohn- und Eßraum ein Arbeitszimmer, ein Schlafzimmer mit Duschraum und Toilette sowie die Küche.

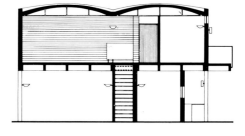

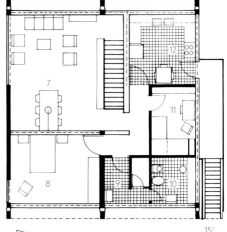

15'
5 m

1. View from south-west. Concrete frame and brick panelling are clearly contrasted. The lunettes below the concrete roof vaults provide top lighting.

2–4. Section, upper floor plan and ground floor plan. Key: 1 Car port, 2 Tools, 3 Spare room, 4 Shower bath and WC, 5 Entrance and main stairs leading to upper floor, 6 Back stairs leading to kitchen, 7 Living-cum-dining room, 8 Bedroom, 9 Shower bath, 10 WC, 11 Study, 12 Kitchen.

5. General view, with the dramatic background of the landscape.

6. Hilltop view of the rear of the house, with a concrete shell roof and continuous clerestory lighting of the north side.

7. Ground floor entrance with the main stairs, consisting of wooden steps placed on steel bars firmly held between wall panels. Behind the pebble-faced wall on the right is the spare room.

1. Ansicht von Südwesten. Betonrahmen und Backsteinausfachung sind deutlich voneinander abgesetzt. Segmentförmige Oberlichter unter den Betonschalen.

2–4. Querschnitt, Grundrisse von Wohngeschoß und Untergeschoß. Legende: 1 Wageneinstellplatz, 2 Geräte, 3 Gastzimmer, 4 Dusche und WC, 5 Eingang und Haupttreppe zum Wohngeschoß, 6 Nebentreppe zur Küche, 7 Wohn- und Eßraum, 8 Schlafzimmer, 9 Dusche, 10 Toilette, 11 Arbeitszimmer, 12 Küche.

5. Gesamansicht von Südwesten.

6. Blick vom Hang auf die Rückseite mit dem Beton-Schalendach und dem Oberlichtband auf der Nordseite.

7. Hauseingang im Untergeschoß mit der zwischen Wandscheiben verspannten Haupttreppe aus Holzstufen auf Stahlprofilen. Hinter der mit Feldsteinen verkleideten Mauer rechts liegt das Gastzimmer.

8. Living room furniture. The untreated concrete ceiling contrasts with the whitewashed brick panelling, the pebble-faced walls and the inlaid strip floor. The lunettes provide diffused top lighting.
9. Dining area in the living room. Untreated brick walls with different textures.
10. Built-in kitchen with ceramic flooring.

8. Sitzgruppe im Wohnraum. Oberflächenkontraste von schalungsrauh belassener Decke, weiß gestrichener Backsteinausfachung, Wandverkleidung aus Feldsteinen und Langriemenparkett. Ausgeglichene Belichtung durch Oberlichtsegmente.
9. Eßecke im Wohnraum. Natur belassene Backsteinwände in verschiedener Texturierung.
10. Einbauküche mit Fußboden aus Keramikmosaik.

**House at Pride's Crossing,
Massachusetts**

Architects: Lawrence, Shannon & Underwood, Boston, Massachusetts

**Ferienhaus in Pride's Crossing,
Massachusetts**

Architekten: Lawrence, Shannon & Underwood, Boston, Massachusetts

This house, situated on the Massachusetts North Shore, is mainly intended for summer use. It stands on a narrow, almost bare strip of land which climbs sharply from the Atlantic to a sandy bluff before dropping to a shallow meadow. The house had to be sited at least 100 ft behind the highwater line; but to preserve the sea view, it was placed on 8 ft high concrete piers which had a vital influence on the overall design. On the cruciform plan stands a flat-roofed, exposed timber frame structure which, because of the salt water spray, consists of solid mahogany. Mahogany has also been used for the 4×10 ft plywood wall panels which provide the design module for the entire house.

Dieses an der Nordküste von Massachusetts gelegene Ferienhaus dient hauptsächlich als Sommeraufenthalt. Es ist auf einem fast vegetationslosen schmalen Landstreifen errichtet, der vom Atlantik zunächst in sandigem Gelände ansteigt, um sich dann in eine flache Mulde zu senken. Da das Haus mindestens 30 m hinter die Flutlinie zurückgenommen werden mußte und andererseits die Aussicht auf das Meer erhalten bleiben sollte, wurde es auf 2,44 m hohe Betonpfeiler gesetzt, auf die die Gesamtkonstruktion abgestimmt ist. Auf kreuzförmigem Grundriß wurde eine sichtbar belassene Holzrahmenkonstruktion mit Flachdach errichtet, die wegen des salzhaltigen Sprühwassers der Brandung aus massiven Mahagonibalken erstellt wurde. Die Abmessungen der ebenfalls aus Mahagonisperrholz bestehenden Wandfelder (1,22×3,05 m) dienten als Modul für die Gesamtkonstruktion.

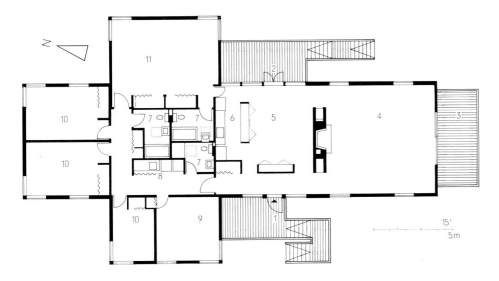

1. (Page 99) North side. Because of the cruciform plan, it was possible to provide all four bedrooms, though they are of different size, with ceiling-high corner windows.
2. South-east side. In the foreground, the longer arm of the cross with the living rooms and the cantilevered, canopy-shaded south terrace, offering a sea view. Below the central part of the main floor are a concrete-enclosed boiler room and storage room.
3. Main floor plan. Key: 1 West terrace with entrance, 2 East terrace, 3 South terrace, 4 Living room with fireplace, 5 Dining room, 6 Kitchen, 7 Bathroom, 8 Recess with washing machine, 9 Library, 10 Bedroom, 11 Master bedroom.
4. West terrace with the main entrance.

1. (Seite 99) Ansicht von Norden. Die Kreuzform des Grundrisses machte es möglich, alle vier Schlafräume trotz unterschiedlicher Größe einheitlich mit raumhohen Eckfenstern auszustatten.
2. Gesamtansicht von Südosten. Im Vordergrund der längere Kreuzarm mit den Wohnräumen und dem auskragenden Südbalkon (Aussicht auf das Meer), der durch eine Kragplatte beschattet wird. Unter der Kreuzzone des Wohngeschosses mit Badezimmern und Küche befinden sich im Untergeschoß zwei gemauerte Sockel (Heizung und Vorratsraum).
3. Grundriß des Wohngeschosses. Legende: 1 Westbalkon mit Eingang, 2 Ostbalkon, 3 Südbalkon, 4 Wohnraum mit Kamin, 5 Eßraum, 6 Küche, 7 Badezimmer, 8 Nische für Waschmaschine, 9 Bibliothek, 10 Schlafraum, 11 Elternschlafraum.
4. Der Westbalkon mit dem Haupteingang.

5. South terrace in front of the living room, with sea view. Timber structure and overhang of solid mahogany units, wall panels of mahogany plywood.
6. West side passage to main living room. Behind the folding door on the left is the recess with the washing machine; behind the cupboard wall are kitchen and dining room, which are separated from the living room area by the fireplace unit.
7. Sitting room with full-height glass doors leading to the south balcony.

5. Der Südbalkon an der Stirnseite des Wohnraums mit Blick auf den Atlantik. Holzkonstruktion und Kragarme des Schutzdaches aus massiven Mahagonibalken, Wandfelder aus Mahagonisperrholz.
6. Westlicher Durchgang zum Hauptwohnraum. Hinter der Falttür links die Waschmaschinennische, hinter dem Wandschrank Küche und Eßraum, der vom Wohnbereich durch den Kaminblock getrennt ist.
7. Der Wohnraum mit den raumhohen Glastüren zum Südbalkon.

House at the beach of Mantoloking, New Jersey

Architect: Marcel Breuer, New York 22, N.Y.
Associate: Herbert Beckhard

Ferienhaus am Strand von Mantoloking, New Jersey

Architekt: Marcel Breuer, New York 22, N.Y.
Mitarbeiter: Herbert Beckhard

This beach house, habitable throughout the year, faces the Atlantic on the east side. As the houses on either side are very close, the north and south sides are almost completely windowless while the east and west sides are glass walls. The building proper stands on columns except for a concrete core containing the ground level entrance, boiler room and maid's room. The greater part of the house rests on a bearing structure, consisting of twin timber beams stained dark-brown, and heavy timber columns. In the centre is the split-level living room; around it are the other rooms, with dining room, kitchen, utility room and study on the main floor, and three bedrooms and two bathrooms on the upper floor. A separate garage is placed on the west side of the house.

Dieses ganzjährig bewohnbare Strandhaus ist nach Osten zum Atlantik hin orientiert. Wegen der dicht angrenzenden Nachbarhäuser sind die Nord- und Südseite fast völlig geschlossen, während die Ost- und Westfassade in Glaswände aufgelöst wurden. Der eigentliche Baukörper ist auf ein Stützen- und Sockelgeschoß gesetzt, dessen Kernzone mit tragenden Betonblockwänden den ebenerdigen Eingang, Heizung und Mädchenzimmer umfaßt. Der Hauptteil des Hauses ruht auf einer Tragkonstruktion aus dunkelbraun gebeizten Doppelbalken und schweren Holzstützen. Zentrum des Hauses ist der durch zwei Geschosse reichende Wohnraum, um den sich die übrigen Räume gruppieren: Eßplatz, Küche, Wirtschaftsraum und Studio im ersten Stock und im Obergeschoß drei Schlafräume und zwei Badezimmer. Eine separate Garage liegt westlich vom Haus.

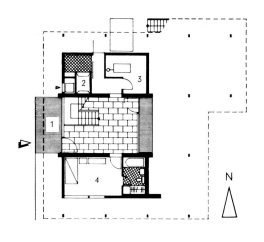

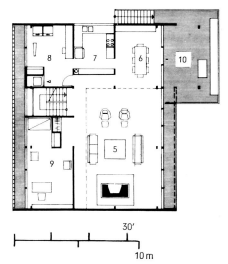

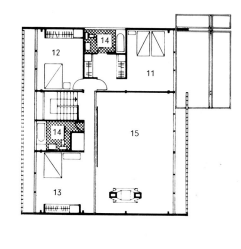

30'

10 m

N

1. East side.
2. Ground floor plan, main floor plan, and upper floor plan: 1 Entrance, 2 Shower room, 3 Boiler room, 4 Maid's room, 5 Living room, 6 Dining room, 7 Kitchen, 8 Utility room, 9 Study, 10 Terrace, 11 Master bedroom, 12 Child's bedroom, 13 Guest room, 14 Bathroom, 15 Upper part of two-storey living room.
3. West side, with sun protection grille.
4. Close-up of the terrace.
5. Living room, seen from the gallery.

1. Gesamtansicht von Osten.
2. Grundriß von Erdgeschoß, Hauptgeschoß und Obergeschoß: 1 Eingang, 2 Duschraum, 3 Heizung, 4 Mädchenzimmer, 5 Wohnraum, 6 Eßplatz, 7 Küche, 8 Wirtschaftsraum, 9 Studio, 10 Terrasse, 11 Eltern, 12 Kinder, 13 Gast, 14 Bad, 15 Oberer Teil Wohnraum.
3. Westseite mit Sonnenschutzgrill.
4. Detailansicht der Terrasse.
5. Wohnraum von der Galerie aus.

1. South side. Below the sun deck on the left is the car port. In the eastern part of the living room the chimney breast of the fireplace.

1. Südfront. Unter der Sonnenterrasse mit Pergola links der Wageneinstellplatz. Im Ostteil des Wohnraums der Kamin.

Beach house in Montauk, Long Island

Architects: Peter Blake and Alan Chapman, New York City, N.Y.

Because of the risk of erosion this beach house had to be set well back from the coast; but on the other hand it was desired to obtain a sweeping sea view. The living room was therefore placed on the upper floor while the lower floor contains two bedrooms and two bathrooms. The south front of the living room is completely glazed. Part of the kitchen section has been screened off by partitions. The chimney, built up from ocean-worn rock, also serves the master bedroom on the lower floor. A glass sliding door gives access to the large sun deck which is shielded from the road by translucent, white corrugated plastic panels. The timber structure, with panels of vertically or diagonally placed boards, stands on a concrete block foundation. The design is based on a module of 4 × 4 ft.

Strandhaus in Montauk, Long Island

Architekten: Peter Blake und Alan Chapman, New York City, N.Y.

Das Strandhaus mußte der Erosionsgefahr wegen von der Steilküste abgerückt werden, andererseits sollte es eine möglichst umfassende Aussicht auf den Atlantik bieten. So wurde der Wohnraum in das Obergeschoß verlegt, und im Untergeschoß wurden zwei Schlafräume und zwei Badezimmer untergebracht. Die Südfront des Wohnraumes ist voll verglast. Der Küchenbereich wurde teilweise durch Zwischenwände abgeteilt. Der Kamin aus Natursteinen, die von der Brandung abgeschliffen wurden, hat eine zweite Feueröffnung im Elternschlafraum des Untergeschosses. Durch eine Glasschiebetür gelangt man auf das große Sonnendeck, das mit gewellten Platten aus durchscheinendem weißem Kunststoff gegen die Straße abgeschirmt ist. Die Holzkonstruktion, die mit vertikal oder diagonal angeordneten Holzbrettern ausgefacht wurde, steht auf einem Sockel aus Betonblocksteinen. Dem Entwurf liegt ein Modul von 4 × 4 Fuß zugrunde.

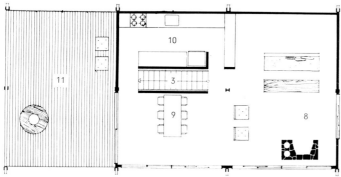

2. The north façade (from the back) clearly shows the 4×4 ft module. Above the wall panels are glazed strips with pivoted openings.
4. View from the living room on the sun deck which provides a view of the Atlantic.

2. Die Nordseite (Rückfront) läßt den Planungsmodul von 4×4 Fuß erkennen. Über den Wandfeldern Fensterbänder mit Klappflügeln.
4. Blick vom Wohnraum zum Sonnendeck mit Sicht auf den Atlantik und die Steilküste.

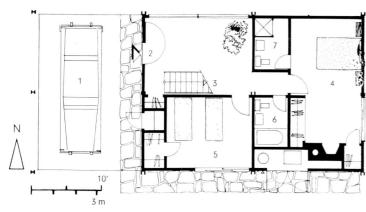

3. Upper and lower floor plans. Key: 1 Car port, 2 Entrance, 3 Staircase, 4 Master bedroom, 5 Bedroom, 6 Bathroom, 7 Shower bath, 8 Living room, 9 Dining area, 10 Kitchen, 11 Sun deck.

3. Grundrisse von Ober- und Untergeschoß: 1 Wageneinstellplatz, 2 Eingang, 3 Treppenhaus, 4 Elternschlafraum, 5 Schlafraum, 6 Bad, 7 Duschraum, 8 Wohnraum, 9 Eßplatz, 10 Küche, 11 Sonnendeck.

Twin houses at Aspen, Colorado

Architect: Charles S. Sink, Denver, Colorado

The two houses, erected on a steep north slope about 300 ft above the winter sports centre of Aspen, can be reached from a car park in the valley by a funicular. The timber structure rests on concrete pile foundations which extend below the depth of frost penetration. The buildings are raised on twin columns so high that, even in deep snow, the two houses are well clear of the ground. By the exposed roof joists and the stanchions, the interior is divided into four bays of equal size. The bay at the north-eastern end contains two double-bedrooms; the one next to it the service unit consisting of kitchen, WC and bathroom. The third bay with the living-cum-dining room can be combined with the bedroom in the fourth bay by removing a folding partition. From the balcony a flight of stairs leads to the roof terrace.

Zwillings-Ferienhäuser in Aspen, Colorado

Architekt: Charles S. Sink, Denver, Colorado

Die beiden Ferienhäuser, die auf einem steilen Nordhang etwa 100 m über dem Wintersportzentrum Aspen errichtet wurden, sind von einem tiefer gelegenen Parkplatz mit einer Zahnradbahn zu erreichen. Die Holzkonstruktion ruht auf Pfahlgründungen aus Beton, die bis unter die Frostgrenze reichen. Doppelstützen heben die rechteckigen Baukörper so hoch über das Gelände, daß die beiden Häuser auch bei tiefem Schnee frei über dem Terrain stehen. Durch die sichtbaren Deckenbalken und die freistehenden Vertikalstützen wird der Innenraum in vier gleichgroße Felder unterteilt. Das erste Feld auf der Nordostseite umschließt zwei Doppelschlafzimmer, dann folgt die Naßzelle mit Küche, Toilette und Bad. Das dritte Feld mit dem Wohn- und Eßbereich kann durch Zurückschieben einer Faltwand mit dem Schlafteil in der vierten Achse kombiniert werden.

1. West side. On the left the covered track of the funicular. The ground level core contains the heating installation. Creosoted structure, redwood wall panels.
2. North-west elevation. In the two centre bays, the twin stanchions are braced by wires.
3. On the north-west side, facing the valley, a balcony extends along one half of the house. From it, a flight of stairs leads along the side wall up to the roof which is used as a sun deck throughout.
4. Plan. Key: 1 Entrance, 2 Living room, with island fireplace, 3 Dining area, 4 Bedroom which can be separated by a folding partition, 5 Kitchen, 6 WC, 7 Bathroom, 8 Bedroom, 9 Bedroom with sleeping bunks, 10 Balcony, 11 Stairs to sun deck.
5. Sitting room with dining area. Between the stanchions is the rear wall of the service unit.

1. Gesamtansicht von Westen. Links die überdachte Zahnradbahn. In den zurückgesetzten Blöcken unter den Hauskuben ist die Heizungsanlage untergebracht. Holzkonstruktion dunkelbraun geteert, Wandfelder mit Rotholzausfachung.
2. Ansicht von Nordwesten. In den beiden mittleren Achsen sind die Doppelstützen mit Drahtseilen diagonal verspannt.
3. Auf der Nordwestseite zum Tal hin ist vor die eine Haushälfte ein Balkon gesetzt. Von hier führt auf der Schmalseite eine Treppe auf das Dach, das als Sonnendeck benutzt wird.
4. Grundriß. Legende: 1 Eingang, 2 Wohnbereich, mit freistehendem Kamin, 3 Eßplatz, 4 durch Faltwand abtrennbarer Schlafraum, 5 Küche, 6 WC, 7 Bad, 8 Schlafraum, 9 Schlafraum 10 Balkon, 11 Treppe zum Sonnendeck.
5. Wohnraum mit Eßplatz. Zwischen den freistehenden Stützen die Naßzelle.

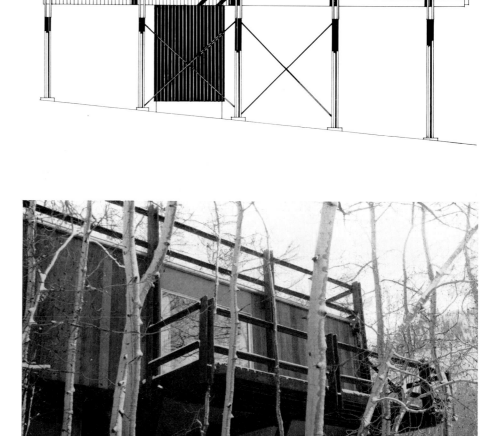

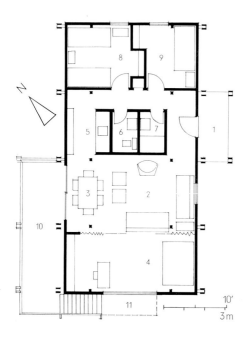

1. South-west side of the largely transparent house; the wall panels between the projecting beams are extensively glazed.

1. Südwestseite des weitgehend transparenten Baus, dessen Wandfelder zwischen freiliegenden Bindern großenteils voll verglast sind.

House near Seattle, Washington

Architect: Wendell H. Lovett, Bellevue, Washington

Ferienhaus bei Seattle, Washington

Architekt: Wendell H. Lovett, Bellevue, Washington

Because of the view, this two-storey house faces north-east; it stands on a wind-swept slope in a region of woods and lakes to the east of Seattle. The elegant lightness of its structure is reminiscent of aircraft design. The wood frame with its twinned Douglas Fir beams and posts rests on concrete and pumice block foundations. The plan is a simple rectangle. The lower floor, at garden level and partly dug into the slope, contains a bedroom, study, hobby room, bathroom, WC and utility room; on the upper floor are the living room, two bedrooms, bathroom and kitchen. With its compact, economic room arrangement and projecting roof beams, the house conveys the impression of a friendly shelter, despite the transparency of the structure.

Dieses zweigeschossige, der Aussicht wegen nach Nordosten orientierte Ferienhaus, das auf einem Bergrücken im wald- und seenreichen Gebiet östlich von Seattle steht, erinnert in der eleganten Leichtigkeit seiner Konstruktion an den Flugzeugbau. Das Holzskelett mit spantenartig ausgesparten Trägern und Stützen aus Douglastannenholz ruht auf einem Sockel aus Bimsbetonblöcken. Der Grundriß ist ein einfaches Rechteck: Auf gleichem Niveau mit dem Garten und halb in den Hang eingegraben liegt das Untergeschoß, zu dem ein Schlafzimmer, ein Arbeitszimmer, ein Bastelraum, Bad und WC sowie ein Wirtschaftsraum gehören, während das Obergeschoß den Wohnraum, zwei Schlafzimmer sowie Bad und Küche umfaßt. Durch die kompakte, kostensparende Anordnung der Innenräume und die weit auskragenden Dachbinder entsteht ein Eindruck der Geborgenheit, der mit der Transparenz des Konstruktionsgerüstes kontrastiert.

2. Cross-section, with north-west side of living room.

3. East side. Wood frame construction with cedarwood facing over plywood and vertical studs.

4. View from the living room towards the master bedroom from which it is separated by a cupboard unit. The twinned roof beams and in fact the entire timber structure are painted white.

5. Main floor and lower floor plans. Key: 1 Entrance, 2 Bedroom, 3 Study, 4 Hobby room, 5 Utility room, 6 Bathroom, 7 Sitting room, 8 Dining area, 9 Kitchen, 10 Balcony.

2. Querschnitt mit Nordwestseite des Wohnraums.

3. Ansicht von Osten. Holzrahmenkonstruktion an den Stirnseiten mit Zedernholzschalung über Sperrholztafeln und senkrechten Pfosten.

4. Blick vom Wohnraum zum Elternschlafraum, dazwischen Schrankelement als Raumteiler. Die spantenartig ausgesparten Deckenbalken wie die ganze Holzkonstruktion weiß gestrichen.

5. Grundriß von Hauptgeschoß und Untergeschoß: 1 Eingang, 2 Schlafraum, 3 Arbeitsraum, 4 Bastelraum, 5 Wirtschaftsraum, 6 Bad, 7 Wohnraum, 8 Eßplatz, 9 Küche, 10 Balkon.

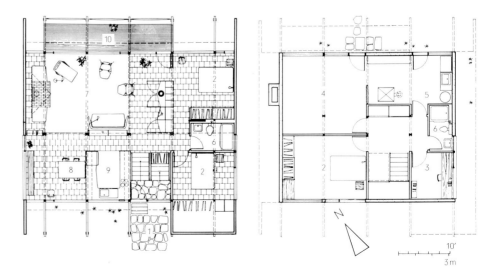

Mountain lodge at Thredbo, New South Wales, Australia

Architect: Harry Seidler, Sydney

This lodge stands at the edge of a ski resort village high up in the Australian Snowy Mountains. Its three floors are divided longitudinally so that, on each floor, one half of the house is a few steps lower than the other. The shape of the compact timber building is determined by the requirements which call for the floor areas to increase towards the top. The comparatively small lower floor, constructed of rubble walling, contains a ski room, sauna, wash and drying rooms. On the intermediate level are two double bedrooms and two further bedrooms with four sleeping bunks each. On the deeply overhanging top floor are the sitting rooms and two large sun decks. The projecting floors are supported by a framework of timber trusses. The V-shaped supports are bolted, and stained black.

Berghaus in Thredbo, New South Wales, Australien

Architekt: Harry Seidler, Sydney

Dieses Berghaus steht am Rand eines Skiferiendorfes hoch in den australischen Schneebergen. Seine drei Geschosse sind in der Längsachse geteilt und hälftig um einige Stufen gegeneinander versetzt. Die Form des kompakten Holzbaus ist ganz den Bedürfnissen angepaßt: von unten nach oben vergrößert sich, dem Raumprogramm entsprechend, die Nutzfläche. Das verhältnismäßig kleine, von Natursteinmauern umgebene Untergeschoß nehmen Skiraum, Sauna, Waschküche und Trockenraum ein. Im Mittelgeschoß sind zwei Doppelschlafzimmer und zwei weitere Schlafräume mit je vier Doppelstockbetten untergebracht. Darüber erstreckt sich weit ausladend das Wohngeschoß mit den Aufenthaltsräumen und zwei großen Sonnendecks. Die nach oben immer weiter auskragenden Geschosse werden von einem Gerüst aus Holzbindern getragen; die V-förmig geneigten Stützbalken sind verschraubt und schwarz gebeizt.

1. North-east side. Colours: Grey rubble walling, black stained timber trusses, brown ash board facing. A free spanning 50 ft long plywood ramp leads on the south side into the central main stairway.
2. North side. Behind the strip window of the intermediate floor are the bedrooms; above them between the inclined supports is the sun deck.
3. Entrance and rear side, seen from south-west.

1. Gesamtansicht von Nordosten. Farbgebung: grauer Bruchsteinsockel, schwarz gebeizte Holzbinder, braune Eschenholz-Schalbretter. Eine frei spannende, 15 m lange Sperrholzrampe führt auf der Südseite ins Treppenhaus.
2. Nordseite. Hinter dem Fensterband des Mittelgeschosses Schlafräume, darüber zwischen den Stützen das Sonnendeck.
3. Eingangs- und Rückseite.

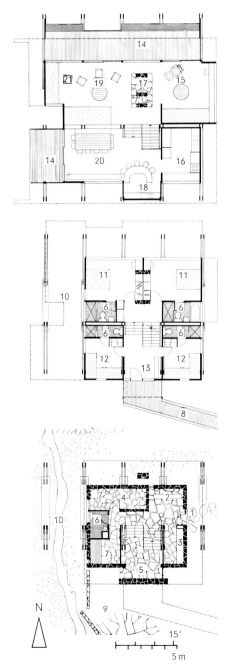

4. Plan of lower floor (bottom), intermediate floor (centre) and upper floor (top). Key: 1 Ski entrance, 2 Ski room, 3 Store room, 4 Wash and drying room, 5 Entrance from car park, 6 Shower bath and bathroom, 7 Sauna, 8 Access ramp, 9 Car park, 10 Mountain creek below the projecting part of the building, 11 Bedroom, 12 Room with four sleeping bunks, 13 Ramp entrance, 14 Sun deck, 15 Sitting area, 16 Kitchen, 17 Fireplace with two openings, 18 Bar, 19 Sitting room, 20 Dining area, 21 Glass panel in the floor, giving a view of the creek.

4. Grundriß von Untergeschoß (unten), erstem Obergeschoß (Mitte) und zweitem Obergeschoß (oben). Legende: 1 Skiläufereingang, 2 Skiraum, 3 Vorratsraum, 4 Waschküche und Trockenraum, 5 Eingang vom Parkplatz her, 6 Duschraum/Badezimmer, 7 Sauna, 8 Zugangsrampe, 9 Parkplatz, 10 Bach unter dem auskragenden Teil des Hauses, 11 Schlafzimmer, 12 Raum mit vier Schlafkojen, 13 Rampeneingang, 14 Sonnendeck, 15 Sitzecke, 16 Küche, 17 Kamin mit zwei Feuerstellen, 18 Bar, 19 Wohnraum, 20 Eßplatz, 21 Glasplatte zum Durchblick auf den Bach.

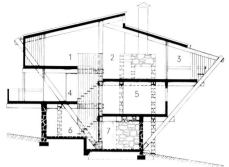

5. East side, seen from the access ramp. The stagger of the floor levels and the increase in floor area from one floor to the next are clearly apparent.
6. Cross section. Key: 1 Dining room, Kitchen and bar, 2 Sitting room, 3 Sun deck, 4 Ramp entrance and rooms with sleeping bunks, 5 Bedrooms, 6 Entrance from car park, 7 Ski entrance, store room and sauna.
7. West side. On this side, as a result of the differences in floor area, the only enclosed part near the supports in the foreground is the living room on the top floor.
8. View from the kitchen towards the dining area and the west balcony on the higher level of the living room floor. Here, a clerestory window provides additional daylight. On the right, on a lower level, the remaining part of the living room with the glass sliding doors leading to the sun deck.
9. Steps leading from the lower part to the higher part of the living room, with kitchen, bar and dining area.
10. Sitting room corner and fireplace.

5. Blick von der Zugangsrampe auf die Ostfassade. Die Versetzung der Geschoßebenen ist deutlich zu erkennen. Auch die Vergrößerung der Nutzfläche von Stockwerk zu Stockwerk läßt sich an den Auskragungen ablesen.
6. Querschnitt. Legende: 1 Eßraum, Küche und Bar, 2 Wohnraum, 3 Sonnendeck, 4 Rampeneingang und Räume mit Schlafkojen, 5 Schlafzimmer, 6 Eingang vom Parkplatz, 7 Skiläufereingang, Vorratsraum und Sauna.
7. Ansicht von Westen. Die allseitige Abstufung des Baukörpers führte auf der Westseite dazu, daß in der vordersten Stützenachse nur die Wohnebene im zweiten Obergeschoß ausgebaut ist.
8. Blick von der Küche aus auf Eßplatz und Westbalkon im höher gelegenen Teil des Wohngeschosses. Ein schmaler Oberlichtstreifen sorgt für zusätzliche Belichtung dieser Zone. Rechts der tiefer liegende Wohnbereich mit der Glasschiebetür zum Sonnendeck.
9. Aufgang vom Wohnraum zum höher gelegenen Teil mit Küche, Bar und Eßplatz.
10. Blick aus der Sitzecke auf den Kamin.

House at Rovio, Ticino

Architects: Tita Carloni and Luigi Camenisch, Lugano

The house stands on the San Vigilio hill near Rovio at an altitude of approximately 1,600 ft. Because of the hard porphyry subsoil, covered by a relatively thin layer of humus, the architects tried to adapt the building as far as possible to the contours of the site in order to avoid costly earthworks. The rooms are therefore arranged in steps so that no excavations were required. The façades are designed in large diagonal patterns arranged at the same angle as the slope (30°). The rough masonry base has been constructed by local masons in the time-honoured local tradition so that the house is in architectural sympathy with a Romanesque chapel further down. The interior is covered by shell-like wooden panelling.

Ferienhaus in Rovio, Tessin

Architekten: Tita Carloni und Luigi Camenisch, Lugano

Das Haus steht auf der Kuppe von San Vigilio bei Rovio in etwa 500 m Höhe. Der besonders harte Porphyruntergrund, der nur von einer verhältnismäßig dünnen Humusschicht bedeckt ist, veranlaßte die Architekten, den Baukörper weitgehend der natürlichen Geländeform anzupassen, um kostspielige Aushubarbeiten zu vermeiden. Hieraus folgte eine stufenförmige Anordnung der Räume unter Verzicht auf eine eigentliche Baugrube. Die Fassadenflächen sind in großen Diagonalen angeordnet, die mit einem Gefälle von 30° parallel zu den Berg- und Hügellinien geführt wurden. Das Haus besteht aus einem Unterbau aus Natursteinen, den einheimische Maurer als Kopfmauerwerk nach einem seit altersher ortsüblichen Verfahren errichteten, so daß das neue Haus und eine etwas weiter unten liegende romanische Kapelle eine architektonische Einheit bilden. Die schalenartige Holzüberdeckung umschließt den Innenraum.

1. South side, showing the way in which the house is arranged in steps so as to follow the slope. The lower part, built of traditional local rubble walling, is in keeping with the Romanesque chapel in the foreground (right).

2. Section A-A (top), section B-B (centre) and plan (bottom). Key: 1 Pergola, 2 Living room, 3 Sitting area with fireplace, 4 Dining area, 5 Entrance, 6 Kitchen, 7 Children's bedroom, 8 Master bedroom, 9 Bathroom and WC, 10 Oil heater, 11 Basement.

3. South side, with pergola. Walls, window openings and roof areas reflect the 30° angle of the slope.

1. Gesamtansicht von Süden mit dem in Stufen der Hangneigung folgenden Baukörper, dessen Bruchsteinsockel in der Mauertechnik der örtlichen Tradition entspricht, wie sie schon die romanische Kapelle im Vordergrund rechts zeigt.

2. Schnitt A–A (oben), Schnitt B–B (Mitte) und Grundriß (unten). Legende: 1 Pergola, 2 Wohnraum, 3 Kamin, 4 Eßplatz, 5 Eingang, 6 Küche, 7 Kinderschlafzimmer, 8 Elternschlafzimmer, 9 Bad und WC, 10 Ölofen, 11 Keller.

3. Die Südseite mit der Pergola. Mauern, Fensteröffnungen und Dachflächen entsprechen mit ihren 30°-Winkeln dem Gefälle.

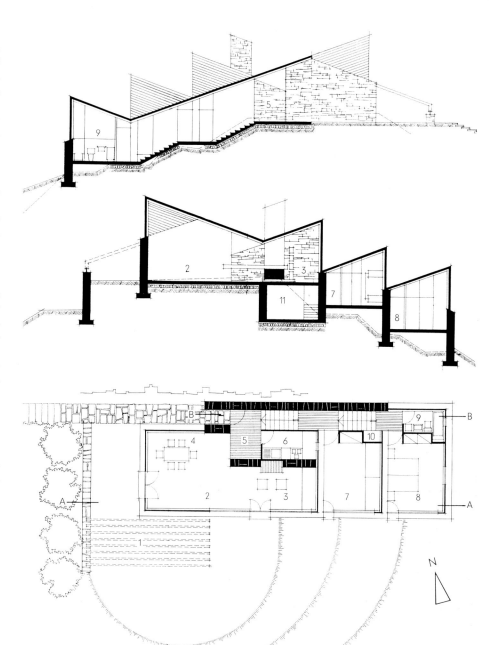

4. Children's bedroom. Because of the sloping roof, the upper beds leave ample space for those sleeping below.

4. Das Kinderschlafzimmer. Die oberen Doppelstockbetten lassen wegen des schrägen Dachanstiegs reichlich Platz.

5. The enclosed part on the west side contains the large living room.
6. Interior of living room.
7. The view from north-east shows the north wall which, but for minute window openings, is almost wholly enclosed, and the three shed-like superstructures with their narrow vertical windows, projecting from the sloping roof.
8. Outdoor sitting area under the pergola.

5. Der geschlossene Bauteil auf der Westseite umfaßt den großen Wohnraum.
6. Blick in den Wohnraum.
7. In der Nordostansicht wird die bis auf wenige kleine Fensteröffnungen geschlossene Nordmauer und die glatte Dachfläche sichtbar, aus der die drei shedähnlichen Dachaufbauten mit ihren schmalen Fensternischen herausragen.
8. Freisitzplatz unter der Pergola.

Twin cottages at San Martino di Castrozza (Trento)

Architects: Angelo Mangiarotti and Bruno Morassutti, Milan

These twin cottages, completely identical in arrangement and plan, are staggered by the depth of one house. Construction and materials are in keeping with traditional local practice; coarse rubble walling, round timber bearing structure of firwood, tongued and grooved deal boarding. In the interior, too, the rustic note has been consistently maintained. The centre of each house is formed by the large L-shaped living room at ground floor level which, in the sitting room area, extends through two storeys right up to the roof and is, through the dining corner, directly connected with the kitchen behind the fireplace unit. The three bedrooms on the upper floor are reached from the sitting room gallery. On the lower floor is a maid's room, boiler room, and covered porch open to the south which is used by the children as a summer playground.

Zwillings-Ferienhäuser in San Martino di Castrozza (Trient)

Architekten: Angelo Mangiarotti und Bruno Morassutti, Mailand

Die Zwillings-Ferienhäuser, die sich in Raumprogramm und Grundriß genau gleichen, sind um Haustiefe gegeneinander versetzt. Konstruktion und Material entsprechen der in den Dolomiten traditionellen Bauweise: grobes Mauerwerk aus Natursteinen, tragende Holzstruktur aus Tannen-Rundhölzern und gespundete Schalung aus Tannenbrettern. Auch im Inneren ist die rustikale Note konsequent durchgehalten. Das Zentrum jedes Hauses bildet der große, L-förmige Aufenthaltsraum im Erdgeschoß, der im Wohnteil durch zwei Stockwerke bis unter das Dach reicht und über den Eßplatz direkt mit der Küche hinter dem Kaminblock verbunden ist. Die drei Schlafräume im Obergeschoß sind über die Galerie des Wohnraums zugänglich. Das Souterraingeschoß umfaßt das Mädchenzimmer, den Heizungsraum und eine gedeckte, nach Süden offene Halle.

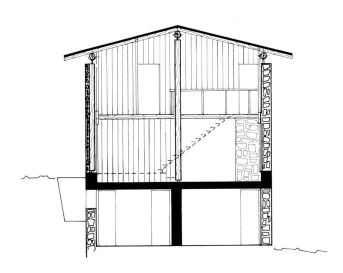

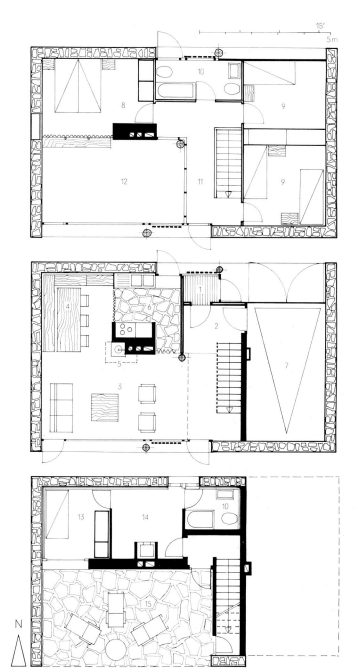

1. South-west side. Between the solid wall panels is the large glass front of the living room, facing south; because of the horizontal partition, the two-storey living room is not recognizable as such from outside.
2. Cross-section of basement, ground floor and upper floor.
3. Plans of basement (bottom), ground floor (centre) and upper floor (top). Key: 1 Entrance and porch, 2 Hall, 3 Sitting room, 4 Dining corner, 5 Fireplace, 6 Kitchen, 7 Garage, 8 Master bedroom, 9 Children's and guest room, 10 Bathroom and WC, 11 Gallery, 12 Upper space of sitting room, 13 Maid's room, 14 Boiler room, 15 Open porch.
4. At night, the front framing of the living room with the vertical slats of the blinds more clearly visible.

1. Ansicht von Südwesten. Zwischen massiven Wandscheiben die verglaste Südseite des Wohnraums, dessen doppelte Geschoß-höhe wegen der Horizontalteilung von außen nicht erkennbar ist.
2. Querschnitt durch Souterrain und Wohngeschosse.
3. Grundrisse von Souterrain (unten), Erdgeschoß (Mitte) und Obergeschoß (oben). Legende: 1 Eingang und Windfang, 2 Diele, 3 Wohnbereich, 4 Eßplatz, 5 Kamin, 6 Küche, 7 Garage, 8 Eltern-schlafzimmer, 9 Kinder- und Gästezimmer, 10 Bad und WC, 11 Galerie, 12 Luftraum über dem Wohnteil, 13 Mädchenzimmer, 14 Heizung, 15 offene Halle.
4. Bei Nacht treten an der Wohnraumfront die Rahmenfelder mit den vertikalen Holzstablamellen deutlicher hervor.

5. Apart from the window of the master bedroom, the east side of both houses consists of solid rubble walling. The triangular area below the gable roof is glazed. Roof structure consisting of round timbers (fir) covered with deal boards and zinc sheeting.

6. Two-storey living room. On the right the dining corner, above it the gallery with the master bedroom, which can be curtained off from the living room. By night, the two-storey window can be covered by a red curtain.

7. View from the gallery outside the master bedroom past the fireplace chimney towards the entrance side of the living room. Behind the lattice screen are the stairs leading to the upper floor. The door on the gallery leads to the children's room. Apart from the rough-cast and whitewashed fireplace, all the inside walls are either covered by untreated boards or left in coarse rubble walling.

8. View from the dining area towards the rough-cast corner fireplace. On the left the kitchen receives daylight through a large north window.

5. Bis auf das Fenster des Elternschlafraums wurde die Ostwand beider Häuser als massive Bruchsteinmauerscheibe ausgeführt. Das Giebeldreieck unter dem Satteldach ist verglast. Dachkonstruktion aus Tannenrundhölzern mit Tannenbrettern und Zinkblecheindeckung.

6. Blick in den zweigeschossigen Wohnraum. Rechts der Eßplatz, darüber die Galerie mit dem Elternschlafraum, der mit einem Vorhang gegen den Wohnraum abgeschlossen werden kann. Vor die zweigeschossige Fensterwand wird nachts ein roter Vorhang gezogen.

7. Blick von der Galerie vor dem Elternschlafraum am Schornstein des Kamins vorbei auf die Eingangsseite des Wohnraums. Hinter der Lattenwand die Treppe zum Obergeschoß. Die Tür auf der Galerie führt in das Kinderzimmer. Außer dem verputzten und weiß getünchten Kamin sind alle Innenwände mit Naturholz verschalt oder in rohem Bruchsteinmauerwerk belassen.

8. Blick vom Eßplatz auf den verputzten Eckkamin. Links die Küche, die durch ein großes Nordfenster belichtet wird.

Weekend house at Shipton-under-Wychwood, Oxfordshire, England

Architects: Roy Stout and Patrick Litchfield, London

This house stands on the edge of a Cotswold village. It consists of eight separate, single-story units linked with each other by low flat-roofed passages. The plan is opened up fanwise. The separate units form angles of 90° with each other. All of them have single-pitch roofs where, in keeping with local tradition, the eaves gutters are held by the fascias; the latter also form containers for the metal security blinds which protect the all-glass fronts when the house is unoccupied. The almost fully enclosed rear and side walls are of coarse rubble walling. As the rear walls of the units are not at right-angles to the other three, the ridges are sloping, giving rise to interesting visual relationships not easily realised from the geometric clarity of the plan.

Wochenendhaus in Shipton-under-Wychwood, Oxfordshire, England

Architekten: Roy Stout und Patrick Litchfield, London

Das Wochenendhaus liegt am Rande eines Dorfes der englischen Cotswolds. Es besteht aus acht getrennten, eingeschossigen Wohneinheiten, die durch niedrige, flachgedeckte Trakte miteinander verbunden sind. Der Grundriß der Anlage ist fächerförmig aufgelockert. Die einzelnen kleinen Häuschen sind um 90° gegeneinander verdreht. Sie haben sämtlich die ortsüblichen Pultdächer mit der Traufe längs des Stirnbalkens, in dem auch die Metallrolläden untergebracht sind, die in unbewohnten Zeiten die vollverglasten Vorderfronten schützen. Die fast völlig geschlossenen Rück- und Seitenmauern bestehen aus grobem Bruchsteinmauerwerk. Da die Rückwände nirgends im rechten Winkel zu den angrenzenden Wänden stehen, ergeben sich fallende Firstlinien und interessante räumliche Beziehungen, wie sie der klar gegliederte Grundriß nicht ohne weiteres vermuten ließe.

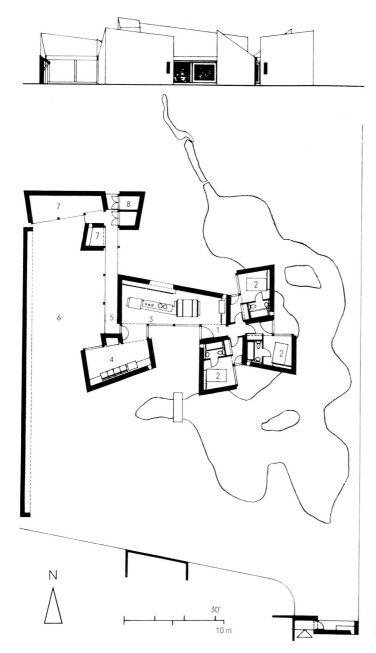

N

30'
10 m

1. East side, with the covered outdoor sitting area, connected with the kitchen area and the living room by a covered passage. In the corner unit on the extreme left is one of the bedrooms, next to it the kitchen and dining area.
2. South elevation (top) and plan. Key: 1 Entrance, 2 Bedroom with cupboard corridor and bathroom, 3 Kitchen and dining area, 4 Living room, 5 Covered passage, 6 Patio, 7 Covered sitting area, 8 Store room.
3. North side, with passage and outdoor sitting area.
4. East side, with two bedroom units and entrance corridor.

1. Blick von Osten auf den überdeckten Sitzplatz, der durch den gedeckten Gang mit dem Küchenbereich und dem Wohnraum verbunden ist. Im Eckhaus ganz links befindet sich ein Schlafraum, daneben der Küchen- und Eßtrakt.
2. Ansicht von Süden (oben) und Grundriß. Legende: 1 Eingang, 2 Schlafraum mit Schrankflur und Bad, 3 Küche mit Eßplatz, 4 Wohnraum, 5 gedeckter Gang, 6 Gartenhof, 7 überdeckter Sitzplatz, 8 Abstellraum.
3. Nordseite mit Gang zwischen Abstellräumen und Freisitzplatz.
4. Ostseite mit zwei »Schlafhäusern« und Eingangskorridor.

5. View southwards from the large, covered outdoor sitting area towards the living room with its tower-like chimney.
6. Corner of the Japanese-style courtyard outside the kitchen and dining room, seen from the south. The single-pitch roofs are boarded, battened, glasswool insulated, and covered with stone tiles.
7. View from the full-height living room window onto the large covered outdoor sitting area in the north-west corner.

5. Blick vom großen gedeckten Freisitzplatz nach Süden auf den Wohnraum mit seinem turmartigen Schornstein.
6. Die Ausbuchtung des nach japanischen Vorbildern gestalteten Gartenhofs vor dem Küchen- und Eßbereich, von Süden gesehen. Die Pultdächer sind sämtlich mit Steinziegeln gedeckt (darunter Lattung auf Brettschalung mit Isolierschichten aus Glaswolle).
7. Blick aus dem raumhohen Fenster des Wohnteils auf den großen gedeckten Sitzplatz in der Nordwestecke.

8. Living room. The roof rafters are left visible in all the rooms. The brickwork backing of the stone walls is, on the inside, painted white. Floors are brown quarry tile with electric underfloor heating.

9. Dining room and kitchen, with the entrance to the living room in the background.

8. Der Wohnraum. Die Holzsparren der Dachkonstruktion wurden in sämtlichen Innenräumen sichtbar belassen. Die Schalenwände aus Ziegelsteinen hinter den Bruchsteinmauern sind im Inneren weiß getüncht. Brauner Fliesenfußboden mit elektrischer Heizung.

9. Eßplatz und Küche, im Hintergrund der Zugang zum Wohnraum.

Beach house on Fire Island, New York

Architects: Charles Gwathmey and
Richard Henderson, New York 23, N.Y.

On the fairly congested beach of Fire Island, a plot of 75 ft × 100 ft was available for a
house which was to be built to a small budget. On this plot, the architects erected a
'fortress' where the occupants are shielded against the outside world by shingled
walls. To obtain the sea view, the main floor is raised about 6 ft above ground. The plan
resembles a swastika. The central living-cum-dining area is flanked by four towers which
contain bedrooms, kitchen and bathroom. The corner towers are, in their turn, flanked by
open sun decks of different sizes which open up towards north, east, south and west. The
occupants are therefore able to be outdoors, in the sun or in the shade, at any time of the
day without having to leave the house. The space below may later be converted into a
guest room or playrooms.

Strandhaus auf Fire Island, New York

Architekten: Charles Gwathmey und
Richard Henderson, New York 23, N. Y.

Für ein Ferienhaus, das keine zu hohen Kosten verursachen sollte, stand in der ziemlich
dicht bebauten Strandzone von Fire Island ein Grundstück von 23 × 30 m zur Verfügung.
Die Architekten errichteten darauf eine »Festung«, deren geschlossene Schindelwände die
Bewohner gegen die Außenwelt abschirmen. Der Aussicht wegen ist das Wohngeschoß
etwa 1,80 m vom Terrain abgehoben. Sein Grundriß hat die Form eines Hakenkreuzes:
An den zentralen Wohn- und Eßraum schließen sich vier Türme an, in denen Schlafräume, Küche und Bad untergebracht sind. Die Eckpfeiler werden ihrerseits von offenen
Sonnendecks verschiedener Größe flankiert, die nach allen vier Himmelsrichtungen ausgreifen. So kann man zu jeder Tageszeit in der Sonne oder im Schatten im Freien sitzen,
ohne das Haus verlassen zu müssen. Das Sockelgeschoß soll später ausgebaut werden.

1. North-east view. The markedly cubist plasticity of the building is accentuated by light and shade; tower-like corners with lean-to roofs rising towards the centre of the house; sun decks jutting like pulpits into the open, and stairs which, in the architect's words, 'wrap around the house like protecting arms'.
2. The sun deck on the north side is the only one not to have its own flight of stairs. It is here that the fortress-like character of the house is particularly apparent.
3. South side. Behind the narrow clerestorey window is the kitchen; the corner tower on the right contains two bedrooms. All four sun decks are connected to the living room area by full-height glass sliding doors.
4. North-west view. Between the corner towers, the flat roof above the central living room is visible.

1. Gesamtansicht von Nordosten. Licht und Schatten akzentuieren die starken plastischen Volumen dieses Baukörpers: turmartige Eckbauten mit Pultdächern, die zum Hauszentrum hin ansteigen, Sonnendecks, die wie Kanzeln in den Außenraum ausgreifen, und Treppen, die sich nach den Worten des Architekten »wie schützende Arme um das Haus legen«.
2. Das Sonnendeck auf der Nordseite hat als einziges keine Außentreppe.
3. Ansicht von Süden. Hinter dem schmalen Oberlichtband die Küche, im rechten Eckturm zwei Schlafräume. Sämtliche vier Sonnendecks sind mit dem zentralen Wohnraum durch raumhohe Glasschiebetüren verbunden.
4. Ansicht von Nordwesten. Zwischen den Ecktürmen ist die horizontale Deckenplatte über dem zentralen Wohnraum zu erkennen.

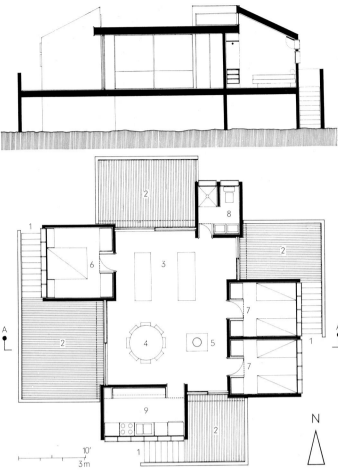

5. Sun deck with shingled walls to ensure privacy.

6. Section A-A and plan of upper floor. Key: 1 External stairs, 2 Sun deck, 3 Living room area, 4 Dining area, 5 Fireplace, 6 Master bedroom, 7 Bedroom, 8 Bathroom and WC, 9 Kitchen.

7. One of the three external stairs leading to the sun decks.

8. A surprising contrast to the fortress-like appearance of the building is the bright interior which opens up on all four sides to full-height glass sliding doors leading to the sun decks. The lateral stagger of the decks creates a diagonal movement of interior space. The external cladding of cedar wood shingles is continued along the walls of the living room. The corner tower seen in the centre contains the master bedroom.

9. Dining area and kitchen beyond. Shingled walls, wooden ceiling.

10. Bedroom. The window can be covered by folding shutters.

11. Interior of the kitchen. Note the clerestory lighting between the lean-to roof and the edge beam of the living room roof.

5. Sonnendeck mit Schindelbrüstung als Sichtschutz.

6. Schnitt A-A und Grundriß des Obergeschosses. Legende: 1 Außentreppe, 2 Sonnendeck, 3 Wohnbereich, 4 Eßplatz, 5 Kamin, 6 Elternschlafraum, 7 Schlafraum, 8 Bad und WC, 9 Küche.

7. Eine der drei Außentreppen zu den Sonnendecks.

8. Bei dem burgartig wirkenden Außenbau überrascht der lichte Innenraum, der sich auf allen vier Seiten durch raumhohe Glasschiebetüren auf die Sonnendecks öffnet. Die seitliche Versetzung dieser Decks ergibt im Innenraum diagonale Bewegungszüge. Die Außenverkleidung aus Zedernholzschindeln ist an den Wänden des Wohnraums kontinuierlich weitergeführt. Der Eckturm in der Bildmitte umschließt das Elternschlafzimmer.

9. Blick auf Eßplatz und Küche. Schindelwände, Holzriemendecke.

10. Schlafraum. Fensterband durch Klappläden verschließbar.

11. Blick in die Küche. Unter dem Pultdach über dem Randbalken der Wohnraumdecke zusätzliche Belichtung durch Fensterband.

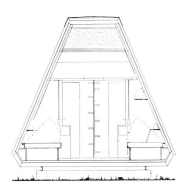 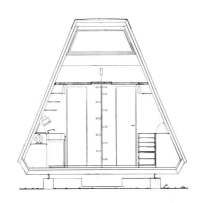 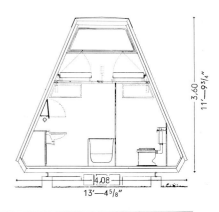

Prefabricated hut

Design: Giulio Minoletti, Milan

This electrically heated 'Capanna Minolina' is a prefabricated miniature hut for four people which is so well insulated that it can also be used as ski hut. The hut can easily be moved to another place. On a brick foundation stands the superstructure which is about 12 ft high and covers a floor area of approximately 170 sq ft. The walls consist of colour-varnished double steel sheeting with an insulating layer of polyurethane foam. The four wall panels correspond to the partitioning inside. The front half of the hut is occupied by the sitting room, which has two tip-up beds; the third bay contains a closet and kitchenette; in the rear bay is the washroom with hip bath and a separate WC. Two further beds are placed on a mezzanine floor covering the rear part of the hut.

Vorfabriziertes Klein-Ferienhaus

Entwurf: Giulio Minoletti, Mailand

Die elektrisch beheizte »Capanna Minolina«, ein vorfabriziertes Kleinst-Ferienhaus für vier Personen, ist so gut isoliert, daß sie auch als Skihütte benutzt werden kann. Da sie einfach zu transportieren ist, besteht die Möglichkeit eines Platzwechsels. Auf einem Sockel aus Ziegelsteinen steht der 3,62 m hohe Aufbau, der eine Grundfläche von rund 16 m² einnimmt. Die Wände bestehen aus farbig lackiertem, doppeltem Stahlblech mit einer Zwischenlage aus Polyurethanschaum zur Wärme- und Schallisolierung. Den vier Wandfeldern entspricht die Raumaufteilung: Die vordere Haushälfte umfaßt den Tages-raum mit zwei Klappbetten, das dritte Feld nimmt Garderobe und Kochnische auf, und in der vierten Achse liegt ein Waschraum mit Sitzbadewanne und ein getrenntes WC. In einem Zwischengeschoß über der hinteren Haushälfte sind zwei weitere Betten unter-gebracht.

130

1. Cross-sections of sitting room (left), kitchenette and closet (centre), and bathroom/WC (right).
2. Side view. The wall panels correspond to the indoor zones. The entrance is protected by a removable awning.
3. Plan. Key: 1 Entrance, 2 Sitting room, 3 Tip-up beds, 4 Closet, 5 Kitchenette, 6 Ladder leading to mezzanine floor, 7 Wash basin, 8 Hip bath, 9 WC.
4. Closet and wash room, seen from the sitting room. (In this case, bathroom and WC occupy opposite positions to those shown in the plan.) The ladder leads to a trap door with two wings, each of which carries a bed. The mezzanine is open towards the sitting room.
5. 'Capanna Minolina' used as a ski hut. The glazed entrance door and the side window can be protected by a wooden shutter. Above the entrance are the rods for the awning.
6. Kitchenette; behind it, the WC.

1. Querschnitte durch Aufenthaltsraum (links), Kochnische und Garderobe (Mitte) und Bad/WC (rechts).
2. Seitenansicht. Die Wandfelder entsprechen den Raumzonen im Inneren. Über dem Eingang ein aufsteckbares Sonnensegel.
3. Grundriß. Legende: 1 Eingang, 2 Aufenthaltsraum, 3 Klappbetten, 4 Garderobe, 5 Kochnische, 6 Sprossenleiter zum Zwischengeschoß, 7 Waschbecken, 8 Sitzbadewanne, 9 WC.
4. Blick aus dem Wohnraum auf die Garderobennische und den Waschraum. (Hier gegenüber dem Grundriß Bad und WC seitenvertauscht.) Die Leiter führt zu einer Falltür, auf deren beiden Flügeln je ein Bett montiert ist. Zum Wohnraum hin ist das »Zwischengeschoß« offen.
5. Die Capanna Minolina als Skihütte. Vor die verglaste Eingangstür und das Seitenfenster kann ein Holzladen geklappt werden. Über dem Eingang das Gestänge für das Sonnensegel.
6. Die Kochnische, dahinter das WC.

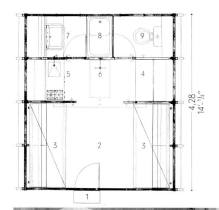

House at Ponte Vedra Beach, Florida

Architect: Robert C. Broward, Jacksonville, Florida

The client required a house which, although perched on the beautiful dunes, would not disturb them. Moreover, the house was to be 'hurricane-proof', ie it was required to resist the Atlantic storms. The house in fact suffered no damage from the hurricane 'Dora' which, in September 1964, otherwise caused widespread damage in Jacksonville and Ponte Vedra. The architect designed an A-frame trusswork of Florida pine which is anchored into the sand dune with wood piling, penetrating 10 ft into the dune. The deep double-pitched roof forms the windowless side walls, which enclose the house entirely on the north and south. Even the west side has relatively small windows, while the east side is all of plate glass, affording an ocean view. The cantilevered sun deck in the centre is protected from being overlooked from the beach by an inclined end wall.

Ferienhaus am Strand von Ponte Vedra, Florida

Architekt: Robert C. Broward, Jacksonville, Florida

Das Strandhaus sollte sich nach dem Wunsch des Bauherrn vollkommen in die Dünenlandschaft einfügen, außerdem sollte es »hurricane-proof« sein, d. h. es mußte den atlantischen Wirbelstürmen widerstehen können. Tatsächlich hat es den Hurrikan »Dora«, der 1964 Ponte Vedra verheerte, unbeschädigt überstanden. Der Architekt entwarf eine A-förmige Fachwerkkonstruktion aus Pinienholz, die er zum Schutz gegen Sturmfluten mit Holzpfählen 3 m tief im Dünensand verankerte. Das weit herabgezogene Zeltdach bildet die fensterlosen Seitenwände, die das Haus vollkommen abschließen. Auch die Westfassade hat relativ kleine Fenster, während die Ostfront mit ihren großen Glasflächen den Blick auf den Ozean freigibt. Das in der Mittelachse des Hauses weit auskragende Sonnendeck ist durch seine abgeschrägte Stirnwand gegen Einblick vom Strand geschützt.

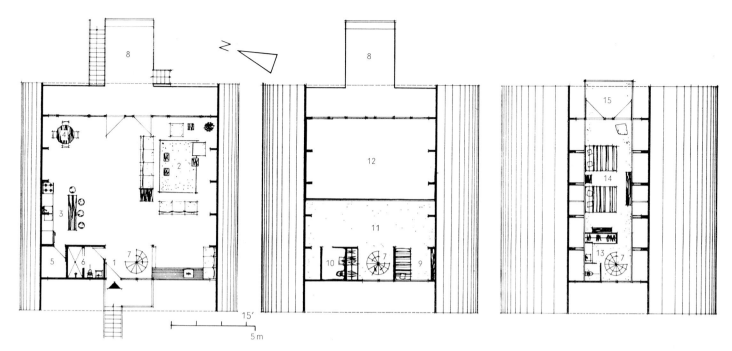

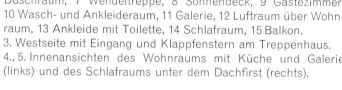

1. The window front facing the beach. The ridge rises 43 ft above floor level. Wall facings and roof shingles are of pine.
2. Plans of ground floor, first floor and second floor: 1 Entrance, 2 Sitting room, 3 Kitchen, 4 Dining area, 5 Store room, 6 WC and shower bath, 7 Spiral stairs, 8 Sun deck, 9 Guest room, 10 Wash and dressing room, 11 Gallery, 12 Air space above living room, 13 Dressing room with WC and washbasin, 14 Master bedroom, 15 Balcony.
3. West side with main entrance and staircase windows.
4, 5. Interiors of living room with kitchen and gallery (left) and master bedroom under the ridge (right).

1. Die verglaste Strandseite. Firsthöhe 13,20 m über Fußbodenoberkante. Wandschalungen und Dachschindeln aus Pinienholz.
2. Grundrisse Erdgeschoß, 1. und 2. Obergeschoß: 1 Eingang, 2 Wohnraum, 3 Küche, 4 Eßplatz, 5 Vorratsraum, 6 Toilette und Duschraum, 7 Wendeltreppe, 8 Sonnendeck, 9 Gästezimmer, 10 Wasch- und Ankleideraum, 11 Galerie, 12 Luftraum über Wohnraum, 13 Ankleide mit Toilette, 14 Schlafraum, 15 Balkon.
3. Westseite mit Eingang und Klappfenstern am Treppenhaus.
4., 5. Innenansichten des Wohnraums mit Küche und Galerie (links) und des Schlafraums unter dem Dachfirst (rechts).

1. Off-shore side with sun deck. Glass sliding door leading to the sitting room. Timber structure, shingled roof, inside facing of wood strip. Thermal insulation adequate for winter habitation. Oil-fired hot air heating.
2. Plans of ground floor and attic: 1 Sun deck, 2 Living room, 3 Dining area, 4 Kitchen, 5 WC and shower bath, 6 Bedrooms.

1. Landseite mit Sonnendeck. Glas-Schiebetür zum Wohnraum. Holzkonstruktion, Schindeldach, Innenschalung mit Holzleisten. Winterfeste Isolierung. Ölbefeuerte Warmluftheizung.
2. Grundrisse von Erdgeschoß und Dachgeschoß: 1 Sonnendeck, 2 Wohnraum, 3 Eßplatz, 4 Küche, 5 WC und Dusche, 6 Schlafräume.

House on the north coast of Zealand, Denmark

Architect: Ole Hagen, Copenhagen

The house stands on the cliffs of the Kattegat coast, about 100 ft above sea level. Because of its wind-swept position, the house has been given the shape of a tent, with sloping roofs taken down to the floor slab. The latter rests on a low, retracted base of rubble walling which, built as a basement, contains the necessary utility rooms. Inside, the long sides of the house are formed by the sloping roofs, the short sides by Thermopane glass walls. The U-shaped living area at ground floor level surrounds the brick core of kitchen, WC and fireplace. Dining area and sitting room proper face the sea; on the off-shore side, in the lee of the house and partly covered by the tent roof, the floor slab is projected as a sun deck. An attic under the central part of the roof has sleeping accommodation for four people.

Ferienhaus in Nord-Seeland, Dänemark

Architekt: Ole Hagen, Kopenhagen

Das Haus steht direkt an der Steilküste des Kattegatts, etwa 30 m über dem Meer. Wegen der ungeschützten, stark dem Wind ausgesetzten Lage wurde es in Zeltform entworfen, mit Dachschrägen, die bis zur Bodenplatte herunterreichen. Diese ruht auf einem niedrigen, zurückgesetzten Sockel aus Natursteinen, der – als Keller ausgebaut – die nötigen Wirtschaftsräume enthält. Das Hausinnere wird auf den Längsseiten von den Dachschrägen und an den Giebelseiten von Glaswänden aus Thermopanescheiben begrenzt. Der Wohnbereich im Erdgeschoß legt sich U-förmig um den gemauerten Kern mit Küche, WC und Kamin. Eßplatz und Sitzgruppe sind zur Seeseite orientiert, während landeinwärts, im Windschatten des Hauses die Bodenplatte als Sonnendeck auskragt. Unter dem First wurde ein Zwischengeschoß mit vier Schlafgelegenheiten eingezogen.

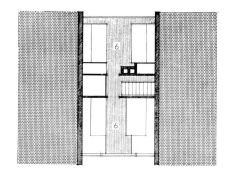

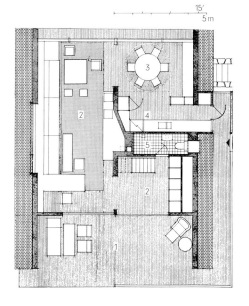

15′
5m

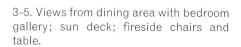

3-5. Views from dining area with bedroom gallery; sun deck; fireside chairs and table.

3–5. Ansichten von Eßplatz mit Schlafgalerie, Sonnendeck und Kaminsitzplatz.

Summer and weekend house in the Landes, France

Architects: Y. Salier and A. Courtois, Bordeaux

Ferien- und Wochenendhaus in den Landes, Frankreich

Architekten: Y. Salier und A. Courtois, Bordeaux

This house stands in a clearing in the wooded region of the Landes, about 40 miles from Bordeaux. It has the shape of a flat pyramid on a square plan. With its deep roof, covered with greenish slate, the house conveys the impression of a shelter – an impression reinforced by the fact that the floor is about 3 ft below ground level. The interior is a single room; one-quarter of which is taken up by the service unit with kitchen, heating, wash room and shower bath. The lower ends of the pinewood rafters remain visible and represent an important architectural feature, forming a kind of pergola surrounding the house.

Das Ferien- und Wochenendhaus liegt auf einer Waldlichtung in den Landes, etwa 60 km von Bordeaux entfernt. Es hat die Form einer flachen Pyramide über quadratischem Grundriß. Das tief herabreichende, mit grünlichen Schieferplatten gedeckte Dach gibt ihm den Charakter einer schützenden Zuflucht inmitten des Waldes, ein Eindruck, der noch dadurch verstärkt wird, daß der Fußboden 90 cm unter Geländeniveau liegt. Das Innere besteht aus einem einzigen Raum, der zu einem Viertel von dem gleichfalls quadratischen, freistehenden Installationsblock mit Küche, Heizung, Wasch- und Duschraum eingenommen wird. Die Sparren aus Tannenholz liegen im unteren Teil des Daches frei und sprechen als sichtbare Konstruktionselemente im Erscheinungsbild des Hauses stark mit. Vor dem Fensterband, das rings um den Innenraum läuft, bilden sie eine Art Pergola.

136

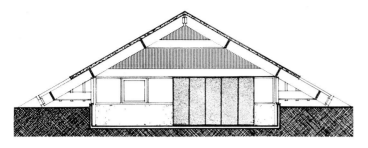

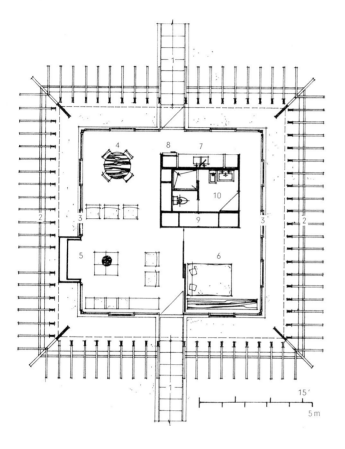

1. The windows of the 'flat pyramid' house are at meadow level. The house has two entrances on opposite sides.
2. Section and plan: 1 Entrance, 2 Rafters, 3 Clerestory window, 4 Dining area, 5 Living room area with fireplace, 6 Dormitory area, 7 Kitchen, 8 Heating, 9 Cupboard walls, 10 Bathroom and WC.
3. The four main trusses are supported by short concrete piers.
4. Dining and sitting area. The rafters are visible through the window.
5. Service unit and the sliding grille partition screening the bedroom are so low that the impression of the unity of the room is not impaired.

1. Die Fenster der flachen Hauspyramide liegen auf gleichem Niveau wie die Waldwiese. Das Haus hat zwei gegenüberliegende Eingänge, zu denen man über einige Betonstufen hinabsteigt.
2. Schnitt und Grundriß: 1 Eingang, 2 Sparrenwerk, 3 Fensterband, 4 Eßplatz, 5 Wohnbereich mit Kamin, 6 Schlafbereich, 7 Küche, 8 Heizung, 9 Wandschränke, 10 Waschraum und WC.
3. Die vier Hauptbinder stützen sich auf Betonpfeiler ab.
4. Eß- und Wohnbereich. Sparrenwerk durch Fenster sichtbar.
5. Installationsblock und Gitterschiebewand (Blickschutz für Schlafbereich) sind so niedrig, daß die Raumeinheit gewahrt bleibt.

House in Squaw Valley, California

Architect: George T. Rockrise, San Francisco

This house, which the architect built for himself, is used throughout the year and so designed that, apart from the architect's own family, there is sufficient room for guests with children. In the design, it was desired to attain privacy, to make the most of the panorama, to achieve maximum economy, and ease of heating. The building has a square plan (32 × 32 ft); it has a part-basement which contains a dormitory, heating plant etc, and two upper floors. The top floor is connected with the living room on the main floor, by means of a gallery. Basement walls and floors are of concrete, all other parts of wood, designed to a module of 4 × 4 ft. The roof is developed into four gables so that snow is dispersed in all directions.

Ferienhaus in Squaw Valley, Kalifornien

Architekt: George T. Rockrise, San Francisco

Das Ferienhaus des Architekten wird ganzjährig benutzt und ist so eingerichtet, daß sich außer der eigenen Familie noch eine Gastfamilie mit Kindern bequem unterbringen läßt. Beim Entwurf wurde besonderer Wert auf Ungestörtheit, gute Aussichtslage sowie auf Sparsamkeit der Mittel und leichte Heizbarkeit gelegt. Das Gebäude, das über quadratischem Grundriß (32 × 32 Fuß) errichtet ist, hat ein teilweise ausgebautes Untergeschoß mit einem großen Schlafraum, Heizungs- und Kellerräumen und zwei Obergeschosse, wobei das höher gelegene über eine Galerie mit dem Wohnraum im Hauptgeschoß in Verbindung steht. Wände und Fußboden des Untergeschosses bestehen aus Beton, die übrigen Teile sind als Holzkonstruktion errichtet, der ein Modul von 4 × 4 Fuß zugrunde liegt. Das Dach ist zu vier Giebeln aufgefaltet, wodurch die Schneelasten nach allen Seiten abgeleitet werden.

1. South side. The gable of the two-storey living room is entirely of glass. On the right, the terrace overlooking the creek, with the outside stairs leading to the basement dormitory.

2. Site plan. The house has been placed so that the strong force of the west winds is broken by the corner of the house. It was also desired to place the house as close as possible to the creek, and as far away as possible from the road. Key: 1 Car park, 2 Barbecue, 3 Playground at the creek, 4 Playing field.

3. Plans of upper floor with gallery (left) and ground floor (right). Key: 1 Entrance with ski store, 2 Living room, 3 Kitchen, 4 Bedroom, 5 Bathroom, 6 Store room, 7 Staircase, 8 Gallery, 9 Air space above living room.

4. Apart from the vertical strip formed by the two windows, the west side gable is enclosed and faced with cedar boards.

1. Ansicht von Süden. Der Giebel des zwei Geschosse hohen Wohnraums ist ganz verglast. Rechts die Terrasse über dem Wildbach mit der Außentreppe zum Schlafraum im Untergeschoß.

2. Lageplan. Das Haus ist so in das Grundstück gesetzt, daß die starken Westwinde sich an der über Eck gestellten Hauskante brechen. Außerdem sollte es möglichst nahe am Bach stehen. Legende: 1 Parkplatz, 2 Picknickplatz mit Grill, 3 Spielplatz am Bach, 4 Spielfeld.

3. Grundrisse von Obergeschoß mit Galerie (links) und Erdgeschoß (rechts). Legende: 1 Eingang mit Skiablage, 2 Wohnraum, 3 Küche, 4 Schlafraum, 5 Bad, 6 Abstellraum, 7 Treppenhaus, 8 Galerie, 9 Luftraum über Wohnraum.

4. Der Westgiebel ist bis auf den senkrechten Streifen mit den beiden Fenstern geschlossen und mit Zedernholz verschalt.

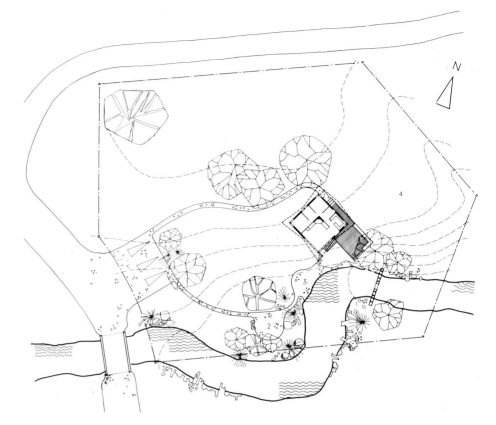

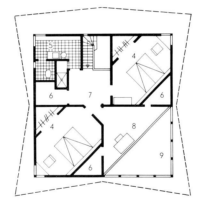
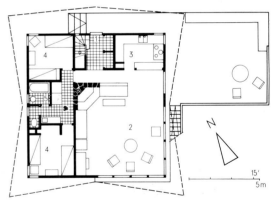

5. View from the gallery in the south corner of the living room. The grilles of the oil-fired hot air heating system can be seen in the floor. The underside of the roof has a cedar wood cladding.
6. Living room with the fireplace built up from concrete blocks. Behind the dining area are the kitchen and the exit to the terrace. The gallery runs diagonally across the living room so that the front half of the latter extends through two storeys.

5. Blick von der Galerie auf die Südecke des Wohnraums. Im Fußboden sind die Auslässe der ölbefeuerten Warmluftheizung zu erkennen. Dachunterseite mit Zedernholzlatten verschalt.
6. Der Wohnraum mit dem Kamin aus Betonsteinen. Hinter dem Eßplatz die Küche und der Ausgang auf die Terrasse. Die Galerie läuft diagonal durch den Wohnraum, der in seiner vorderen Hälfte zweigeschossig ist.

Ski hut in a village resort near Harbor Springs, Michigan

Architect: Henry P. Glass, Chicago

In designing his house, which can accommodate up to twelve people, the architect arrived at a solution which combines compactness with the appearance of loftiness. Moreover, the concentrated two-storey building is highly economical in space utilisation and to heat. The plan has the shape of an equilateral triangle. Over each side rises an 'A' frame which carries the gable roof. The timber structure is externally and internally faced with wood; the roof is shingled. The pointed corners are partitioned off, being used as entrance, kitchen, bathroom and utility room, respectively, so that the central ground floor living room has a hexagonal shape. In a sunken pit, its centre is the open fireplace whose flue extends all the way up through the top of the roof. On the gallery floor are three bedrooms and corresponding cupboard space.

Skihütte in einem Feriendorf bei Harbor Springs, Michigan

Architekt: Henry P. Glass, Chicago

Beim Entwurf seines eigenen Ferienhauses, das bis zu 12 Personen aufnehmen kann, kam der Architekt zu einer Lösung, die zwar das Raumprogramm kompakt zusammenfaßt, aber doch großräumig in der Wirkung ist. Zudem erweist sich der zweigeschossige Zentralbau als sehr ökonomisch in der Flächennutzung und in der Heizung. Der Grundriß hat die Form eines gleichseitigen Dreiecks, über dessen Seiten die A-förmigen Rahmen der Giebelfelder errichtet sind. Die Holzkonstruktion ist außen und innen verschalt, das Dach mit Schindeln gedeckt. Durch Abteilen der Ecken, die als Eingang, Küche, Bad und Hauswirtschaftsraum genutzt werden, bekommt der Wohnraum im Erdgeschoß die Form eines Sechsecks. In seinem Zentrum steht in einer Vertiefung der offene Kamin. Das Galeriegeschoß umfaßt drei Schlafräume und entsprechende Schrankräume.

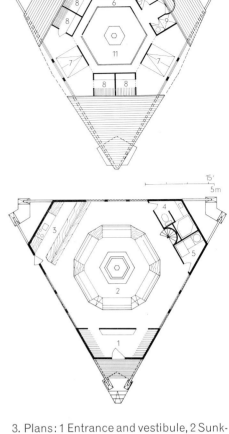

15′
5 m

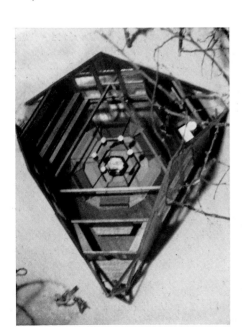

1. (Page 141) The centre of the hexagonal ground floor living room is the sunken pit around the open fireplace. Six benches are grouped around the hearth which can also be used as auxiliary sleeping couches.
2. General view. Above the entrance, the roof is raised to provide snow protection. The 'A' frames rest on concrete supports. Below and above the window panels are ventilating flaps, protected by wood strips.

1. (Seite 141) Zentrum des hexagonalen Wohnraums im Erdgeschoß ist die Sitzgrube mit dem freistehenden Kamin. Um die sechseckige Kaminbank sind sechs Sofas gruppiert, die auch als Behelfsbetten dienen.
2. Gesamtansicht. Über dem Eingang ist das Dach als Schneefang hochgezogen. Abstützung der schrägen Hauptträger auf Betonsockel. Unter und über den festverglasten Fenstern Belüftungsgitter.

3. Plans: 1 Entrance and vestibule, 2 Sunken pit around the fireplace. 3 Kitchen, 4 Bathroom and WC, 5 Utility room, 6 Gallery, 7 Double bedroom, 8 Closet, 9 Shower bath, 10 WC, 11 Air space above fireside pit.
4, 5. Photographs of model, ground floor (left) and gallery floors (right). The photographs clearly show how the space design has been developed from the hexagonal shape of the fireside space. The upper floor gallery permits effective space utilisation even in a vertical direction. Because of the hexagonal plan, there is ample space between the three upper floor bedrooms for easily accessible cupboard room.

3. Grundrisse: 1 Eingang, 2 Kaminsitzgrube, 3 Küche, 4 Bad und WC, 5 Hauswirtschaftsraum, 6 Galerie, 7 Schlafraum, 8 Schrankraum, 9 Duschraum, 10 WC, 11 Luftraum über Kamin.
4, 5. Einblick in das Modell. Links Untergeschoß, rechts Obergeschoß. Die Abbildungen machen deutlich, wie das räumliche Gefüge aus der Sechseckform des Kaminplatzes entwickelt wurde. Die Galerie des Obergeschosses ermöglicht auch in der Vertikalen eine weitgehende räumliche Durchdringung. Durch den hexagonalen Grundriß ergibt sich zwischen den drei Schlafräumen reichlich Platz für begehbare Schrankräume.

142

6. Vestibule with spiral stairs to the upper floor, which had been placed at this point as an afterthought. The entrance door is flanked by a narrow strip of glass; next to it is the folding door to the clothes closet. The windows are large Thermopane panels with permanent sashes. Ventilation is provided by flaps above and below the Thermopane panels which open inwards and are protected on the outside by vertical wood strips. At night, the windows are covered by blinds instead of curtains (of Fig. 1).

7. Kitchen corner, with wall cupboards above the kitchen unit proper. In the foreground the serving counter which also serves as a bar, with a bench having sufficient space for twelve people.

6. Der Vorraum mit der Wendeltreppe zum Obergeschoß, die entgegen dem ursprünglichen Plan hierher verlegt wurde. Neben der Eingangstür schmale Glasstreifen, daneben die Garderobe mit Falttür. Die Fenster sind mit Thermopanescheiben fest verglast. Die Belüftung erfolgt mit Klappflügeln in der Brüstung, die mit Scharnieren nach innen geklappt werden können. Vor den Öffnungen sitzen außen vertikale Holzlamellen. Vor die Fenster werden nachts keine Gardinen, sondern Rollos gezogen (siehe Abbildung 1).

7. Die Küchenecke mit Wandschränken über dem Küchenblock, davor die Anrichte, die auch als Eßplatz dient. An ihren Längsseiten finden zwölf Personen bequem Platz.

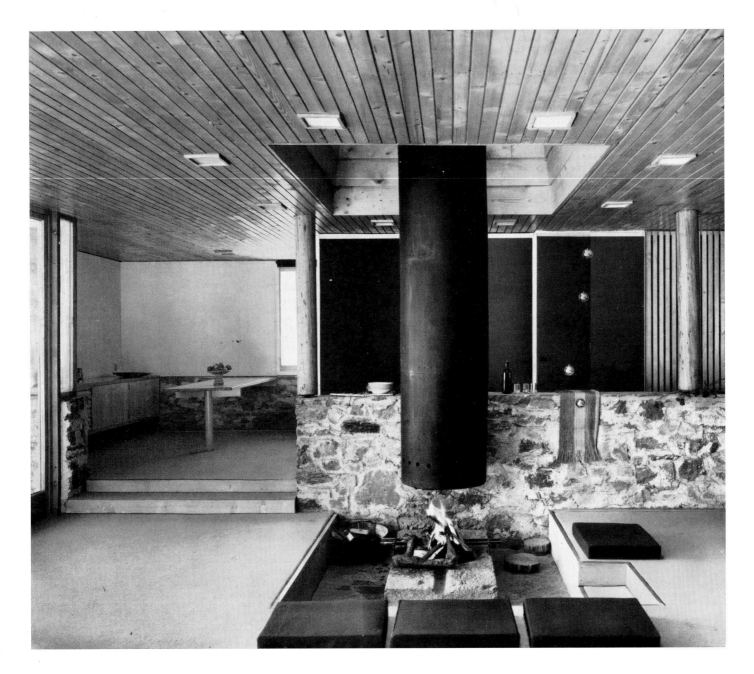

House at San Martino di Castrozza, Italy

Architects: Angelo Mangiarotti and
Bruno Morassutti, Milan

This house in the Dolomites has been erected from traditional local materials, viz rubble walling and fir. The wood has been used as round timbers, as facing battens and boards, and specially treated, white-varnished external facing panels. The square plan corresponds to that of the typical Veneto house: A large central room, extending from north to south, is flanked by two near-symmetrical wings. The east wing comprises three bedrooms and a bathroom, the west wing a spare room, another bathroom, kitchen and dining area. On the south side, the living room is extended to form a loggia with balcony. The centre of the house is the fireplace, which consists of a black-varnished metal flue and is surrounded by an ingle nook. In a basement, made necessary by the sloping ground, are the garages, heating and ancillary rooms.

Ferienhaus in San Martino di Castrozza, Italien

Architekten: Angelo Mangiarotti und
Bruno Morassutti, Mailand

Bei der Konstruktion dieses Ferienhauses in den Dolomiten wurde als ortsübliches Material Bruchstein und Tannenholz verwendet, letzteres als Rundstämme, als Leisten und Bretter zur Verschalung und als spezialbehandelte, weiß gestrichene Paneele am Außenbau. Der quadratische Grundriß entspricht dem Schema des typischen Veneto-Hauses: An einen von Norden nach Süden durchgehenden, großen Mittelraum schließen sich in zwei symmetrischen Flügeln fast spiegelbildlich die Seitenräume an. Der Trakt auf der Ostseite umfaßt drei Schlafräume und ein Bad; an der Westseite liegen ein Gastzimmer, ein weiteres Bad, Küche und Eßplatz. Nach Süden öffnet sich der Wohnraum auf eine Loggia mit Balkon. Zentrum des Hauses ist der Kamin, dessen Blechzylinder von einer Sitzgrube umgeben ist. Im Souterrain liegen Garagen, Heizung und Nebenräume.

1. Living room with open fireplace whose black metal flue extends through a glazed roof opening. On the left the dining area; behind the batten partition is the second bathroom.
2. View lengthwise through the living room which has, on the south side, full-height glass doors leading to the loggia.
5. North side, with entrance and ski room.

1. Der Wohnraum mit dem offenen Kamin, dessen schwarzer Metallzylinder durch ein verglastes Oberlicht geführt ist. Links der Eßplatz, hinter der Lattenwand das zweite Bad.
2. Blick in der Längsrichtung durch den Wohnraum, der sich mit raumhohen Glastüren zur Loggia auf der Südseite öffnet.
5. Gesamtansicht von Norden mit Eingang und Skiablage.

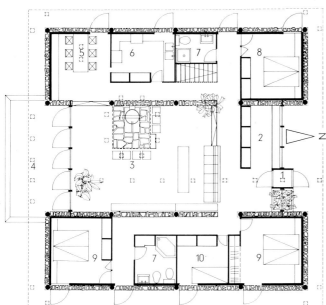

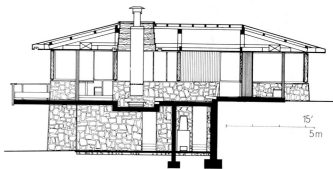

3, 4. Plan and section: 1 Entrance, 2 Closet and ski store, 3 Living room, 4 Loggia, 5 Dining area, 6 Kitchen, 7 Bathrooms, with tub, or shower bath and WC, 8 Guest room, 9 Double bedroom, 10 Single bedroom.

3, 4. Grundriß und Schnitt: 1 Eingang, 2 Kleider- und Skiablage, 3 Wohnraum, 4 Loggia, 5 Eßplatz, 6 Küche, 7 Bad/Dusche und WC, 8 Gastzimmer, 9 Doppelschlafzimmer, 10 Einzelschlafzimmer.

6. Close to the entrance on the north side is a wide hallway which serves as clothes closet and ski store. The cupboards on the left also serve to separate the hallway from the living room. Below the window bench, ski boots can be dried on bars. The floor is covered with large waterproof mats.

7. South side loggia with projecting balcony. Interior and exterior are of the same materials: rubble walling, round timbers, fir wood battens used as facing, and white varnished wall panels.

8. East side, with the bedroom windows. Below the house is the entrance to the basement garages.

9. South side with the projecting balcony. The square boxes, whose glazing is flush with the underside of the ceiling, contain the light fittings. The interior lighting is similar.

6. An den Eingang auf der Nordseite schließt sich ein breiter Gang an, der als Kleider- und Skiablage dient. Die Wandschränke links dienen zugleich als Raumteiler zwischen Vorhalle und Wohnraum. Unter der Bank am Fenster können die Skistiefel auf Stangen getrocknet werden.

7. Die Loggia auf der Südseite mit auskragendem Balkon. Innen- und Außenbau sind mit dem gleichen Material gestaltet: Bruchstein, Rundhölzer, Tannenholzriemen als Verschalung und weiß gestrichene Wandpaneele.

8. Blick auf die Ostseite mit den Fenstern der Schlafräume. Links die Zufahrt zu den Garagen im Untergeschoß.

9. Blick entlang der Südseite. In den quadratischen Kästen, deren Verglasung bündig mit der Deckenunterkante abschließt, sind die Beleuchtungskörper montiert. Auf die gleiche Weise werden auch die Innenräume beleuchtet.

146

House at Camprodón, North Catalonia

Architects: José Antonio Coderch and Manuel Valls, Barcelona

This house for a large family stands in the foothills of the Pyrenees, surrounded by meadows and woods. The simple and clear plan is T-shaped. All bedrooms (master bedroom, plus three double bedrooms for the children) as well as three bathrooms with WCs are in the south-east wing. In the south-west wing is the large sitting room with the covered porch, facing south-east. Adjacent to it, in the north-east wing, is the kitchen, followed by utility rooms, a cloakroom, the maids' room with wash room and WC and, finally, another porch and the garage. The outer walls of the single-storey house are of coarse rubble work which is left exposed on the inside as well. All the window panels and glass doors as well as the open porch outside the living room can be protected by wooden sliding doors.

Ferienhaus in Camprodón, Nordkatalonien

Architekten: José Antonio Coderch und Manuel Valls, Barcelona

Das Ferienhaus für eine kinderreiche Familie liegt von Wiese und Wald umgeben am Fuß der Pyrenäen. Der einfache, klare Grundriß hat die Form eines T. Sämtliche Schlafräume (das Elternschlafzimmer und drei Kinderschlafzimmer mit je zwei Betten) sowie drei Bäder mit WC sind im südöstlichen Flügel untergebracht. Im westlichen Teil des Quertraktes liegt der große Aufenthaltsraum mit der gedeckten, nach Südosten offenen Vorhalle. Im Nordostteil schließen sich Küche und Wirtschaftsräume, eine Garderobe und das Mädchenzimmer mit Waschraum und Toilette sowie eine weitere Vorhalle und die Garage an. Die Außenmauern des einstöckigen Hauses bestehen aus groben Bruchsteinen, die auch im Inneren sichtbar belassen wurden. Sämtliche Fensteröffnungen und Glastüren sowie die offene Halle vor dem Wohnraum können durch Holzschiebetüren geschützt werden.

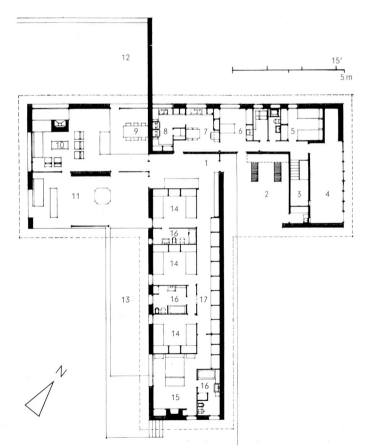

1. (Page 147) View from south-west. In the foreground is the south-west wing with living room and open porch, on the right the bedroom wing. The roof is supported by concrete joists and covered with tiles.

2. Living room with open fireplace, made of sheet iron. The rough stone walls contrast with the whitened ceiling and the palisander wood floor. The glass door on the left leads to the open porch.

3. Plan. Key: 1 Entrance, 2 Garage, 3 Heating, 4 Porch of kitchen wing, 5 Staff bedroom, 6 Cloak room, 7 Utility room, 8 Kitchen, 9 Dining area, 10 Sitting room, 11 Open porch, 12 Patio, 13 Pool of water, 14 Children's bedrooms, 15 Master bedroom, 16 Bathroom and WC, 17 Corridor, fitted with cupboards.

1. (Seite 147) Gesamtansicht von Südwesten. Vorne der westliche Querflügel mit Wohnraum und offener Vorhalle, rechts der Schlaftrakt. Dachstuhl aus Betonträgern mit Ziegeleindeckung.

2. Wohnraum mit offenem Kamin aus Eisenblech. Die groben Steinmauern kontrastieren mit der weißgetünchten Decke und dem Fußboden aus Palisanderholz. Die Glastüre links führt in die offene Vorhalle.

3. Grundriß. Legende: 1 Eingang, 2 Garage, 3 Heizung, 4 Vorhalle Wirtschaftsflügel, 5 Schlafzimmer für das Personal, 6 Garderobe, 7 Hauswirtschaftsraum, 8 Küche, 9 Eßplatz, 10 Wohnraum, 11 offene Vorhalle, 12 Patio, 13 Wasserbecken, 14 Kinderschlafräume, 15 Elternschlafraum, 16 Bad und WC, 17 Schrankflur.

4. The windows and doors on the southwest side of the bedroom wing can be protected against direct sunlight by sliding frames with wooden shutters.
5, 6. The pool of water along the bedroom wing is refreshing on hot days. In this night photograph, the transparency of the living room is particularly striking.

4. Fenster und Türen auf der Südwestseite des Schlaftrakts lassen sich durch Schieberahmen mit Holzlamellen vor direkter Sonneneinstrahlung schützen.
5, 6. Das Wasserbecken vor dem Schlafflügel sorgt an heißen Tagen für Abkühlung. In der Nachtaufnahme läßt sich die Transparenz des Wohnteils besonders deutlich erkennen.

House at Termini di Sorrento, Italy

Architect: Bruno Morassutti, Milan

This 'house under two sails' stands at an altitude of about 1,000 ft above sea level at the tip of the Sorrento Peninsula, facing Capri. Because of the magnificent panorama, the two buildings have been kept mainly transparent. As each of the two roofs rests on four concrete columns, it was possible to provide full-height windows on the sides facing the sun. The rubble stone walling which forms a U-shaped enclosure in the rear of the two parts of the house is separated from the roof by a strip of ventilating windows. Similarly, the cupboard wall partitions stop short of the ceiling. In this way, the interior enjoys excellent cross-ventilation. The backbone of the house is formed by a flight of stone stairs which forms the connection between the two entrances (from the carriageway on the lower level and from the footpath on the upper level) and between the different exteriors.

Ferienhaus in Termini di Sorrento, Italien

Architekt: Bruno Morassutti, Mailand

Das »Haus unter zwei Segeln« liegt 300 m über dem Meeresspiegel am äußersten Ende der Halbinsel Sorrent, gegenüber Capri. Wegen des prachtvollen Panoramas wurden die beiden Baukörper weitgehend transparent gehalten: Da die Dachschalen jeweils auf vier Betonsäulen ruhen, konnten die Fronten zum Meer hin in voller Höhe verglast werden. Die Natursteinwände, die die beiden Hausteile auf der Rückseite U-förmig umfassen, sind durch ein Fensterband mit Klappflügeln vom Dach abgesetzt. Auch die raumteilenden Wandschränke reichen nicht ganz bis zur Decke. Auf diese Weise ergibt sich im Inneren eine ausgezeichnete Querlüftung. Das Rückgrat der Anlage bildet die Steintreppe, die die beiden Zugänge (von der bergab gelegenen Fahrstraße und vom Fußpfad auf der Bergseite her) sowie die verschiedenen Außenräume miteinander verbindet.

1. At night, the structure is clearly apparent: columns of raw concrete; thin concrete dual-curvature shell roof; glass front; rubble walling. In the foreground the main part of the building, with the bedroom on the gallery; on the right, the guest house. In the basement, below the living room, is a further spare room which receives daylight through square windows in the retaining wall.
2. The flight of stairs, following the line of the dip, is protected by the overlapping shell roofs.
3. Plans of main building and guest house, with the gallery floor of the main building on the left: 1 Connecting stairs, 2 Entrance, and access to gallery floor, 3 Living room seats, 4 Dining area, 5 Kitchen, 6 Maid's room and bathroom, 7 Terrace in front of the living room, 8 Guest room, 9 Bathroom for guests, 10 Cupboard corridor, 11 Bathroom, 12 Bedroom, 13 Study, 14 Space above living room.

1. Bei Nacht tritt die Konstruktion deutlich hervor: Sichtbetonsäulen; doppelt gekrümmte, dünne Betondachschale; Glasfront; Naturstein-Mauerscheiben. Vorne das Haupthaus mit dem Schlafteil auf der Galerie, rechts das Gästehaus. Im Sockel unter dem Wohnraum ein weiteres Gästezimmer (durch quadratische Fenster in der Stützmauer belichtet).
2. Die in der Fallinie verlaufende Verteilertreppe.
3. Grundrisse von Haupt- und Gästehaus, links das Galeriegeschoß des Haupthauses: 1 Verbindungstreppe, 2 Eingang und Zugang zum Galeriegeschoß, 3 Sitzgruppe im Wohnraum, 4 Eßplatz, 5 Küche, 6 Mädchenzimmer und Bad, 7 Wohnterrasse, 8 Gästezimmer, 9 Bad für Gäste, 10 Schrankflur, 11 Bad, 12 Schlafteil, 13 Arbeitsplatz 14 Luftraum.

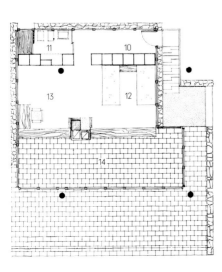

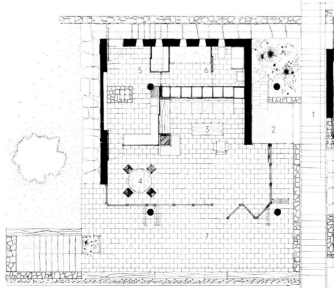

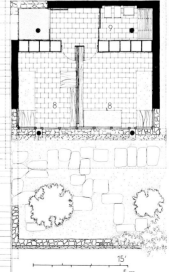

4. View from the main stairs of the two-storey part of the living room, with the bedroom gallery (top, right), fireplace and dining area. The lower part of the glass front, facing the open terrace, can be opened entirely by means of folding doors.
5. View from the terrace across the dining area towards the kitchen area which is distinguished by its bright flooring from the blue-black ceramic tiles of the living room area.
6. Fireplace corner in the living room, below the gallery bedroom.
7. The bedroom on the gallery of the main building. The ventilating windows above the rubble walling are open. Above the cupboard partition on the left, a ventilation gap is provided.
8. View from the bedroom towards the study, likewise situated on the gallery. The shell roof is raised above the concrete columns by bronze fittings, a solution which greatly contributes to the 'floating' appearance of the shell roof. The flue rising from the living room has a second opening on this level. At roof level, the flue is clearly separated from the shell roof and has no contact with it. Floor covered by foam-backed Japanese rush matting.
9. Cross-section of the site, with the main building.

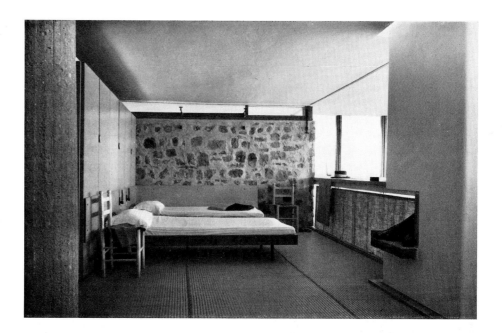

4. Blick von der Zugangstreppe in den zwei Geschosse hohen Teil des Wohnraums mit der Schlafgalerie (rechts oben), Kamin und Eßplatz. Die untere Hälfte der Glasfront läßt sich zur Wohnterrasse hin mit Falttüren völlig öffnen.
5. Blick von der Terrasse über den Eßplatz zum Küchenteil, der durch seinen hellen Bodenbelag vom Wohnbereich mit den blauschwarzen Keramikfliesen abgesetzt ist.
6. Die Kaminecke im Wohnraum unter dem Schlafraum auf der Galerie, von der Terrasse aus gesehen.
7. Der Schlafraum auf der Galerie des Haupthauses. Fensterband mit geöffneten Klappflügeln über der Natursteinmauer. Links Lüftungsschlitz über raumteilender Schrankwand.
8. Blick vom Schlafteil auf den Arbeitsplatz im Galeriegeschoß. Wie hier ersichtlich ist, wird die Dachschale durch Verbindungsstücke aus Bronze von den Betonsäulen abgehoben, eine Lösung, die wesentlich zu dem schwebenden Eindruck der Schalen beiträgt. Der aus dem Wohnraum aufsteigende Kaminblock hat hier eine zweite Feueröffnung. An der Austrittsstelle ist er deutlich vom Dach abgesetzt, das er nirgends berührt. Fußboden: japanische Strohmatte auf Schaumstoffunterlage.
9. Geländeschnitt mit Haupthaus, in dessen Sockel das Gästezimmer zu erkennen ist.

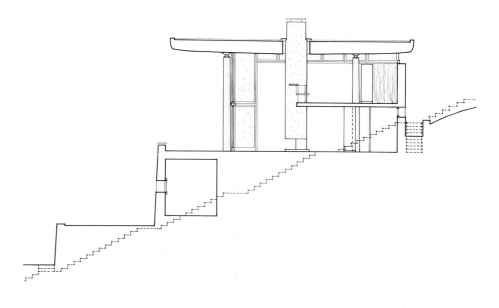

House at Lenno, Lake Como, Italy

Architects: Werner and Grete Wirsing,
Munich
Associate: Rolf Rave

To minimize interference with the landscape and to avoid costly earthworks, this house –
standing 160 ft above the level of the lake and 65 ft below the road – has been placed on
four reinforced concrete stanchions (at about 20 ft centres) anchored into the earth. The
building is stabilised by a strong core of granite rubble walling below the main floor,
which contains the service installations and, in another basement, a bar and wine cellar. The concrete roof and floor slab are supported by cantilevered beams. The roof, projecting 5 ft, is covered with corrugated asbestos cement sheets. A cover tile above the
ridge provides additional cross ventilation. The wholly glazed south side is of alternate
sliding doors and fixed window panels. The other walls consist of two-skin, insulated
panels of pitch pine boards (approximately 10 ft wide) below a strip of windows.

**Ferienhaus in Lenno am Comer See,
Italien**

Architekten: Werner und Grete Wirsing,
München
Mitarbeiter: Rolf Rave

Um die Landschaft möglichst wenig anzutasten und kostspielige Geländeaufschüttungen
zu vermeiden, ist dieses Haus, das 50 m über dem See und 20 m unterhalb der Fahrstraße
liegt, auf vier in den gewachsenen Boden eingespannte Stahlbetonstützen gestellt
(Achsabstand 6 m). Zur Aussteifung ist unter das Wohngeschoß ein massiver Kern aus
Granitbruchsteinen geschoben, der die technischen Anlagen aufnimmt und in einem
weiteren Souterraingeschoß Trinkstube und Weinkeller enthält. Die Betonplatten von
Decke und Fußboden ruhen auf Kragträgern. Das Dach, das 1,50 m auskragt, ist mit Wellasbestzementplatten gedeckt. Die Südwand ist im Wechsel von Schiebetüren und feststehenden Flügeln voll verglast, die übrigen Wände bestehen aus zweischaligen, 3 m breiten Paneelen aus Pitchpinebrettern mit Isolierung, darüber ein umlaufendes Fensterband.

1. View from the car shelter on the east side of the house, and on the wood-panelled rear side.
2. View from the south. The road is above the house. A flight of stairs leads to the bathing beach.
3. South elevation (top), plans of living room floor, service floor and basement. Key: 1 Entrance, 2 Bedrooms, 3 Service unit with bathroom and WC, 4 Kitchen, 5 Dining area, 6 Living room area, 7 Heating room and basement, 8 Covered sitting area with fireside nook, 9 Bar and wine cellar.
4. West side with covered sitting area and fireplace below the living room floor; on the right the stairs leading to the beach, on the left a path leading to the garage.

1. Blick vom Autoeinstellplatz auf die mit Holzpaneelen verkleidete Rückseite.
2. Gesamtansicht von Süden. Über dem Haus die Fahrstraße. Ein Treppenweg führt zum Badeplatz.
3. Ansicht von Süden (oben), Grundrisse von Wohngeschoß, Installationsgeschoß und Untergeschoß. Legende: 1 Eingang, 2 Schlafteil, 3 Installationszelle mit Bad und WC, 4 Küche, 5 Eßplatz, 6 Wohnbereich, 7 Heiz- und Kellerräume, 8 überdeckter Sitzplatz mit Sitzgrube und Kamin, 9 Trinkstube und Weinkeller.
4. Westseite mit Sitzplatz und Kamin unter dem Wohngeschoß, rechts der Treppenweg zum Badeplatz, links der Aufgang zur Garage.

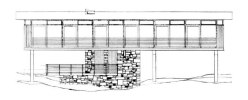

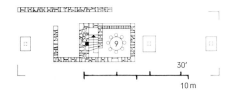

30'
10 m

5. View from the access road on to the western corner of the house. Above the pitchpine panels of the rear wall a continuous strip of windows, and the concrete posts carrying cantilevered concrete joists for floor and roof slabs, can be clearly seen.

6. Underside of living room floor, east side. On the right the rubble walling of the core.

7. View from the house towards the covered car shelter by the road where three cars can be parked.

5. Blick vom Zugangsweg auf den Westteil, über den Pitchpine-Außenwandelementen der Rückseite ist das umlaufende Fensterband gut zu erkennen, ebenso die Betonstütze, von der die Betonbinder für Boden- und Deckenplatte auskragen.

6. Unterseite des Wohngeschosses, Ostteil. Rechts die Bruchsteinmauer des Kerns.

7. Blick vom Haus auf den an der Straße gelegenen Wageneinstellplatz, auf dem drei Autos untergebracht werden können.

8. The living room floor consists of a single coherent space with two cores, viz the service unit, and the fireplace unit next to the stairs leading to the lower floor. Inside the house along the south side is a passage extending along the whole length of the house. By means of sliding doors, the glass front can be opened up the entire length of the house.

9. A view past the granite-walled fireplace towards the sitting area where the end wall is fitted with built-in cupboards of a height corresponding to that of the wall panels. The aperture in the ceiling is part of the hot air heating system; the light fitting is flush with the ceiling. The glass doors can be protected by blinds against excessive sunlight.

10. View of the lake from the bedroom wing which can be subdivided by a collapsible partition. The flooring consists of yellow ceramic tiles throughout.

8. Das Wohngeschoß besteht aus einem einzigen, zusammenhängenden Raum, in den lediglich zwei Festpunkte (die Installationszelle und der Kaminblock neben der Treppe zum Untergeschoß) eingefügt sind. Vor der Südwand ergibt sich im Hausinneren ein langer Gang, der von einer Schmalseite zur anderen reicht. Mit Schiebetüren kann die Glasfront auf die ganze Hauslänge geöffnet werden.

9. Blick an dem aus Granitsteinen gemauerten Kaminblock vorbei auf den Wohnteil, dessen Stirnseite in der Höhe der Wandelemente mit Einbauschränken versehen ist. In der Decke eine Austrittsöffnung der Warmluftheizung und ein bündig liegender Beleuchtungskörper. Die Glastüren können mit Stäbchenrollos gegen zu starke Sonneneinstrahlung geschützt werden.

10. Seeblick vom Schlafteil aus, der durch eine Harmonikawand unterteilt werden kann. Der Fußboden ist durchweg mit gelben Keramikplatten belegt.

House among the Centovalli rocks, Switzerland

Architect: Alfred Altherr, Zurich

On a steep vineyard slope with a view across the Centovalli, a cottage with basement covering in all an area of 5 × 10 metres (16 ft 5 in × 32 ft 10 in), was converted into a house The basement of the old cottage is now used for a garage and workshop, and the ground floor for two bedrooms for parents and sons. The new part of the house consists of a living room resting on the rock, with full-height glass windows facing south and east, followed on the west side by a kitchenette, bathroom, WC and cloakroom. A glass sliding door of the living room gives access to a rock cave with stone bench and table from which a flight of steps hewn into the rock leads to the roof terrace. The natural rock projects into the living room, receding at the 'grotto' and returning once more into the interior next to the main door.

Ferienhaus in den Felsen des Centovalli, Schweiz

Architekt: Alfred Altherr, Zürich

In einem steilen Rebgelände mit Aussicht ins Centovalli wurde eine bereits vorhandene Hütte mit Kellergeschoß von 5 × 10 m Grundfläche zum Ferienhaus ausgebaut. Im Untergeschoß des alten Hauses ist eine Garage und eine Werkstatt eingerichtet, das Erdgeschoß ergab zwei Schlafräume für Eltern und Söhne. Neu hinzugefügt wurde ein an die Felsen angelehnter Wohnraum mit raumhohen Glasfenstern nach Süden und Osten, an den sich westlich eine Küchenbar, ein Bad und WC und eine Garderobe anschließen. Durch eine Glasschiebetür des Wohnraums gelangt man in eine Felsnische mit Steinbank und Tisch, von der eine Treppe im Fels auf die Dachterrasse führt. Der gewachsene Fels ragt stufenweise in den Wohnraum hinein, springt am »Grotto« zurück und wird neben der Haustür noch einmal in das Hausinnere einbezogen.

1. Living room, seen from the east terrace. Dining area and fireplace form a single unit. Cooking facilities are at the table; in the background, on the right, is the 'grotto' with the outdoor sitting area among the rocks.

2. Ground floor plan (top) and floor plan. Key: 1 Cloak room, 2 Bathroom and WC, 3 Kitchen, 4 Living room, 5 Master bedroom, 6 Child's bedroom, 7 Outdoor sitting area among the rocks, 8 Outdoor sitting area in the garden, 9 Garage and workshop, 10 Heating, 11 Guest room.

3. East side with terrace outside the living room annex. Behind it the old cottage which now forms part of the new building.

1. Blick von der Ostterrasse in den Wohnraum. Eßplatz und Kaminblock als Einheit. Feuerstelle und Kochgelegenheit am Tisch, rechts hinten der »Grotto« mit Felsensitzplatz.

2. Grundriß von Erdgeschoß (oben) und Untergeschoß. Legende: 1 Garderobe, 2 Bad und WC, 3 Küche, 4 Wohnraum, 5 Elternschlafraum, 6 Zimmer der Söhne, 7 Felsensitzplatz, 8 Gartensitzplatz, 9 Garage, Werkstatt, 10 Heizung, 11 Gästezimmer.

3. Ansicht von Osten mit der Terrasse vor dem Wohnraumanbau. Dahinter das alte Haus, das in den Neubau einbezogen wurde.

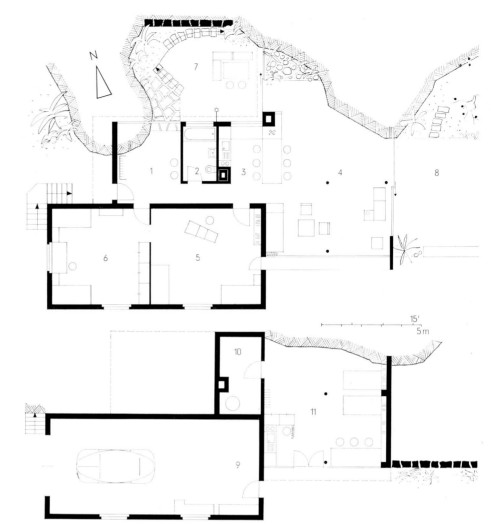

15'
5m

4. The 'grotto', an outdoor sitting area among the rocks, with view across the living room towards the east terrace. The steps hewn into the rock on the left lead to the roof terrace. On the right is the hatch from the kitchen.
5. In the closet adjacent to the main entrance, the natural rock enters the house. Through the window a view of the 'grotto'.
6. Sitting room corner with a view over the valley. Concrete 'deck-chair' with foam rubber mattress, and armchairs designed by the architect. In the background, the east terrace.
7. East terrace, seen from the dining area. On the left, the rock entering the building on which the hammock has been fastened. This photograph shows particularly clearly how the terraced vineyard site has been utilized.

4. Der »Grotto«, ein Freisitzplatz in einer Felsnische mit Blick durch den Wohnraum zur Ostterrasse. Links führen Felsstufen auf die Dachterrasse. Rechts die Durchreiche zur Küche.
5. An der Garderobe neben dem Hauseingang ragt der gewachsene Fels ins Innere. Durch das Fenster Blick in den Grotto.
6. Wohnecke mit Talblick. Liegestuhl aus Beton mit Schaumgummipolster und Sessel nach Entwürfen des Architekten.
7. Blick vom Eßplatz auf die Ostterrasse. Links der in den Innenraum einbezogene Fels, in dem die Hängematte verankert wurde. In dieser Aufnahme wird die Ausnutzung des terrassierten Rebgeländes besonders deutlich.

House and studio in the Centovalli, Switzerland

Architect: Alfred Altherr, Zurich

This house, built by the architect for his own use, stands on a steep slope. The main floor is reached by an external flight of stairs on the west side; here, one first enters the enclosed patio with partly covered outdoor sitting space. Separated by full-height glass walls and a sliding door, the patio leads directly to the central living room which faces south, with a view of valley and mountains. On the mountain side in the north are cloakroom, kitchenette, dining area and bathroom. On the east side follow the bedroom and a morning terrace. On the lower floor, which can only be reached via the external stairs, are a guest room with cooking facilities, WC and shower bath, a basement, and a studio. Construction: The lower floor rubble walling carries a concrete slab, cantilevered on the south side; the upper floor bearing walls and the flat roof are of concrete.

Ferien- und Atelierhaus im Centovalli, Schweiz

Architekt: Alfred Altherr, Zürich

Das eigene Ferienhaus des Architekten liegt an einer steilen Bergflanke. Man betritt das Hauptgeschoß über eine Außentreppe auf der Westseite und gelangt zunächst in den ummauerten Wohnhof mit dem teilweise überdachten Freisitzplatz. Mit raumhohen Glaswänden und einer Schiebetür geht der Wohnhof in den zentralen Wohnraum über, der zugleich auch nach Süden mit Blick über Tal und Berge orientiert ist. Auf der Bergseite, nach Norden, liegen Garderobe, Kochnische, Eßplatz und Bad. Nach Osten schließen Schlafraum und Morgenterrasse an. Das Untergeschoß, das nur über die Außentreppe zu erreichen ist, enthält ein Gastzimmer mit Kochgelegenheit, WC und Dusche sowie Keller und Atelier. Konstruktion: Untergeschoß Bruchstein, darauf eine nach Süden auskragende Betonplatte, im Obergeschoß tragende Wände und Flachdach aus Beton.

162

1. South-west side. Materials and colours of the concrete and glass surfaces of the cantilevered main building are in contrast with the rubble walling of the lower floor.
2. View from the upper slope of the house and the enclosed patio with the gallery, added as an afterthought, leading to the flat concrete roof.
3. The covered southern part of the patio juts out like a pulpit across a former vineyard.
4. Plans of upper floor and lower floor. Key: 1 Entrance, 2 Patio, 3 Hall with cloakroom, 4 Living room, 5 Kitchen, 6 Bathroom, 7 Bedroom, 8 Morning terrace, 9 Porch, 10 Guest room with fireplace and cooking facilities, 11 Studio, 12 Basement.

1. Gesamtansicht von Südwesten. In Material und Farbe kontrastieren die Beton- und Glasflächen des auskragenden Hauptgebäudes mit den Bruchsteinmauern des Sockelgeschosses.
2. Blick vom höher gelegenen Hang auf Hauskörper und vorgeschalteten ummauerten Wohnhof mit der nachträglich aufgesetzten Galerie zu dem flachen Betondach.
3. Der überdachte Südteil des Wohnhofs kragt kanzelartig über den früheren Weinberg aus.
4. Grundriß von Obergeschoß und Untergeschoß. Legende: 1 Eingang, 2 Wohnhof, 3 Diele mit Garderobe, 4 Wohnraum, 5 Küche, 6 Bad, 7 Schlafraum, 8 Morgenterrasse, 9 offene Halle, 10 Gastzimmer mit Kamin und Kochstelle, 11 Atelier, 12 Keller.

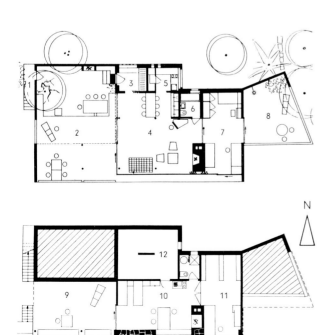

N

5. Patio, seen from the living room. The white-painted wall on the left serves as a projection screen.

6. Living room with view towards bedroom and morning terrace with the sliding partitions open.

7. Above the granite-topped dining table are fluorescent lights, radiating upwards and downwards between limba wood screens. Beyond is the kitchenette.

5. Blick aus dem Wohnraum in den Wohnhof. Die weißgestrichene Fläche links hinten dient als Projektionswand.

6. Der Wohnraum mit Durchblick auf Schlafraum und Morgenterrasse bei geöffneten Schiebewänden.

7. Eßplatz mit Tischplatte aus Granit, darüber nach oben und unten strahlende Leuchtröhren zwischen Blenden aus Limbaholz. Im Hintergrund die Küche.

8. View from the higher part of the patio towards the entrance area which is a few steps lower. In the foreground the concrete table projecting from a bracket; behind it the outdoor fireplace and the concrete brick wall enclosing the patio. The tubular concrete supports of the stools around the cantilevered table are firmly embedded in the smooth soil.

9. Cross-section of patio and the lower floor porch.

10. Night photograph, taken from the patio, with the dining area on the left, the chairs and table facing the rough-hewn granite fireplace on the right, and the passage to the bedroom in the centre.

8. Blick vom höher gelegenen Teil des Wohnhofs auf die um einige Stufen niedrigere Eingangszone. Im Vordergrund der auf einer Konsole auskragende Betontisch, dahinter der Außenkamin und die Hofmauer aus Betonsteinen. Die Betonröhren der Hocker um den Kragtisch sind fest in den Plattenboden eingelassen, die Rundpolster sind abnehmbar.

9. Querschnitt durch den Wohnhof und die Halle des Sockelgeschosses.

10. Die Nachtaufnahme vom Hof aus zeigt links den Eßplatz, rechts vor der Kaminwand aus bruchrauhem Granit die Sitzgruppe, in der Mitte Durchgang zum Schlafraum.

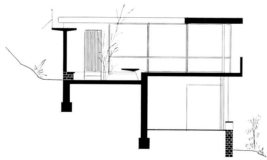

List of Architects

Verzeichnis der Architekten

Photo Credits · Fotonachweis